Looking Through

Rose-Tinted Bifocals

LIGHTHEARTED
VIEWS ON LIFE

ANGELA F. HUSTON

To dear friends
Billie & Erv
Angela F. Huston
(Angie)

Porch Light Press
Sharon Center, Ohio

Published by Porch Light Press P.O. Box 304, Sharon Center, Ohio, 44274, 330/725-4032, crafh@juno.com.

First Edition

10 9 8 7 6 5 4 3 2 1

For the purposes of this book, essays have been slightly edited and some titles have been changed. They do not appear in chronological order but rather are presented according to topic and were published as follows:

"Close the Door When You Leave," originally appeared in *The Cleveland Plain Dealer* (Cleveland, Ohio).

"A Big Lesson From a Little Boy," "As Little Kids Phase Into Adults," "Decor By Any Other Name," "Dignifying the Game of Independence," "In One Year and Out the Other," "It's Finally Time to Play," "Mix 'n Match—Strange Bedfellows," "Some Scents Make No Sense," and "Unconscious Transformation," originally appeared in *Focus* (Akron, Ohio).

"A Coded Reminder of Nomenclature You've Misplaced," "A Place for Everything—In My Purse," "A Thousand Pictures—A Single Word," "It's War Between Man and Squirrel," "Some Firsts Make Lasting Impressions," "Love/Hate Relationships," "Wait! I May Have a Coupon," and "When in Rome, Y'All Listen Carefully," originally appeared in *Horizons* (Wayne County, Ohio).

All other essays originally appeared in *The Medina County Gazette* (Medina, Ohio).

Publisher's Cataloging-in-Publication
(Provided by Quality Books, Inc.)

Huston, Angela F
    Looking through rose-tinted bifocals:
    lighthearted views on life / by Angela F. Huston.
    --1st ed.
    p.cm.
    LCCN: 99-98009
    ISBN: 0-9677085-1-6

    1. Life--Anecdotes.   2. United States-- Social
    life and customs--Anecdotes. I. Title.
    PN6162.H87 2000   818.6
                QBIOO-32 1

WITH LOVE TO
ROSETTE

I FINALLY DID IT, MOM

CONTENTS

Preface   ix

PART I
GIVING MY AGE IN DOG YEARS

The Age Old Question—March 20, 1992   3
Sale-ing Smoothly into Adulthood—October 3, 1995   5
A Big Lesson From A Little Boy—February 1, 1998   8
A Place For Everything—In My Purse—June 1, 1997   11
Don't Do Dumb Things—September 9, 1995   13
Some Scents Make No Sense—July 8, 1997   16
Bugs Assume Right of Eminent Domain—July 16, 1994   18
Shopping: A Little Trip of Horrors—December 2, 1993   21
No Pets Among Peeves—June 24, 1997   23
All For One and One For All—December 28, 1995   26
Melons, Mates, & Other Important Picks—June 30, 1994   29
The Longest Distance Between Two Points
   —January 2,1994   32
Wait! I May Have a Coupon—August 3, 1996   34
It's War Between Man and Squirrel—August 1, 1997   37
A Thousand Pictures—A Single Word—February 3, 1996   40
He Says, She Thinks, They Know—December 18, 1992   43

PART II
COPING WITH THE TECHNOCRATS

A Coded Reminder of Nomenclature You've Misplaced
   —November 29, 1995   49
The Committee is Called to Order—May 26, 1998   52

Do You Speak 0*/$/&>#?—June 10, 1992   54
You are Here—Maybe!—February 9, 1999   57
Mix 'n Match—Strange Bedfellows—May 1, 1996   59
Is There a Lab Rat Assigned to Me?—October 15, 1996   62
Incorporating New Concepts—October 5, 1999   65
Beware of Frozen Fog—December 12, 1995   67
Tattoo Charlie Sees the Big Picture—November 12, 1996 71
Cutting Edge Cooking Gadgets—March 9, 1994   74
An Alarming Situation—November 11, 1997   77
Trespassing in Foreign Territory—November 7, 1992   80
Press Two for Information—March 18, 1997   82
The Facts of Life—Senior Edition—December 9, 1997   85
An Electric Mousetrap—July 11, 1995   88
At the End of My Ribbon—August 8, 1995   91
Blank(et) Statements—June 9, 1998   94

PART III
ENJOYING THE RIDE BETWEEN POTHOLES

Some Firsts Make Lasting Impressions—April 16, 1992   99
When In Rome, Y'All Listen Carefully
    —September 7, 1999   101
Decor By Any Other Name—September 1, 1997   104
Chicken Soup Salvation—February 13, 1996   107
A Woman For All Seasons—January 7, 1997   110
Senior Moments—May 12, 1998   113
A Gap That Won't Be Bridged—March 29, 1993   115
Two Scoops of Common Sense—April 27, 1992   118
Some Questions Have No Answers—January 9, 1996   121
Ask a Silly Question—February 7, 1997   124
How Old is Your Maytag?—April 4, 1995   127
A Personal Perspective on Birds—October 9, 1993   130
Love/Hate Relationships—February 1, 1998   133

The End of the Starter—September 19, 1995   136
Sometimes You'd Better Not Eat Your Wheaties
   —September 8, 1992   139

PART IV
CARRYING MY OWN BAGGAGE

Their Grass Just Looked Greener—April 30, 1996   145
Crossing Lines Between Reality and Optimism
   —February 7, 1995   148
Parenthood is Forever—July 24, 1996   151
As Little Kids Phase Into Adults—September 1, 1996   154
Marriage Discoveries Continue With Age
   —June 27,1995   157
Updating An Old Memory—March 1, 1997   160
The Aging of Wine, Cheese, and Memories—July 21, 1998 163
Upgrading Life Style by Down-Sizing—October 1, 1998   165
In One Year and Out the Other—March 1, 1996   167
Lessons From a Graham Cracker—July 22, 1997   169
Unconscious Transformations—July 1, 1998   172
It's Finally Time to Play—July 1, 1999   175
Chocolate Chip Rewards—May 16, 1995   177
Keeping An Important Connection—August 25, 1998   180
Dignifying the Game of Independence
   —December 16, 1995   182
Close the Door When You Leave—August 20, 1995   184

PREFACE

"Time does not change some things, it ages them well."

The combined experiences of being a daughter, a wife, a mother, and a teacher have provided me with an unlimited supply of anecdotes for my personal kaleidoscope of impressions. Viewing them through rose-tinted bifocals, the sharp edges of some of life's harsh realities are softened. My rose-tinted bifocals also allow me to form workable ways to enjoy, or at least get through, whatever life presents.

I know many of you will identify with this collection of slice-of-life vignettes. My intention in presenting them is to encourage you, as you mature, to maintain enough of your "inner kid" enthusiasm to face newness without abandoning heartfelt nostalgia. Hopefully by doing so, you, too, can create a quiet place between youthfulness and aging—a place where you are always comfortable regardless of chronological age.

I hope, too, the anecdotes remind you of what's *really important*: recognizing and appreciating life's treasures along the way.

ANGELA F. HUSTON

ACKNOWLEDGMENTS

With love and gratitude to my husband Russell and my children Andrew and Ann who always have given me inspiration, encouragement, and support.

For my early columns, I appreciate the help given to me by the following editors: Mary Aaby, Judy Casey, Bill Canacci, David Giffels, John Gladden, Anne Gordon, Janet Fillmore, Jon Kinney, Bill Spoonster, and Paul Workman.

Special thanks to Lavern Hall for guidance, and for helping me keep one foot on the ground when my head was in the clouds.

PART I

Giving My Age
in Dog Years

■ ■ ■

THE AGE OLD QUESTION—MARCH 20, 1992

"Are you an old lady?"

I considered saying, "Not in dog years," but that would have been unfair to my three-year-old friend Kevin. Instead, I honestly said, "Yes." He was temporarily satisfied, although clearly, he was trying to put things in perspective. I understood his confusion.

Age is a number that offers helpful guidelines in our development from infancy to adulthood, but even during those early years confusion often surrounds that number.

Age is a flexible, relative number. To a three-year-old, twelve is light years away; to some young adults, the third and fourth decades suggest impending doom.

While growing up I was frequently told (sometimes on the same day) I was too old or too young to be doing some things. It posed a dilemma; my age was the same, how could that be the reason or excuse for being denied permission! I quickly adopted an attitude characterized by the lyrics of the old song, *You're Either Too Young or Too Old*.

Eventually, age as measured in years ceased to be such a major controlling factor, and I began to learn I could design my life by the way I felt, not by a calendar. As soon as I recognized that, and realized that society actually imposed very few specific age-related requirements—getting a driver's permit or applying for social security—I took control of my life.

Maturity isn't measured in years, as proved by two people I know who approach the age issue with totally different attitudes and results.

I taught with the first in a school where the sixth graders annually challenged the faculty to a volleyball match. There was no question I would participate. One year, however, this new faculty member, a man young enough to be my son, complimented me after the game.

"Wow!" You're *really* good, I'm impressed!"

I had little question where this conversation was headed. I thanked him, adding I firmly believed attitude played an important role in the way one approaches life.

Without hearing what I'd said he persisted.

"I hope I'm in such good condition when I'm your age," then added doubtfully, "but I know I won't be. I'm not in that good a shape now!" Thirty-something and already prepared with an excuse for possible failure in the future.

My instincts urged me to scold him; fortunately, common sense prevailed—he was the new principal! I felt sorry for him, though. His life would be long and unfulfilled unless he readjusted and redirected his attitude.

On the other hand, my friend Billie, (who is twice his age), approaches life with a positive attitude. She believes there are far more worthwhile things to take her attention.

"Why waste precious time fussing over a number that keeps changing anyway? I'm just happy learning, doing, discovering, and enjoying each day," she says, chuckling. Now, that's an attitude ya' gotta love!

A birthday is a day of jubilation, certainly not a time of mourning. Celebrate past successes and anticipate the beginning of another year with a list of new ventures:

- Read all those books you've been putting on hold.
- Plan that trip you've always wanted to take.
- Sign up for a line dancing or aerobics class.
- Resurrect an interest in Canasta in your card club.
- Use jicama in a new recipe without telling guests.

▪ Better yet, enroll in a Sixty Plus (60+) history class at your local state college—you'll delight fellow students with first-hand accounts of the way it *really* was!

I know I still sound like a teacher, but I'm concerned about people whose lives are on hold because a number dictates their activities. It's disturbing to me to see them just sitting and waiting, being swallowed up in little sips of apprehension; some don't even know what they're waiting for.

Everyone has assets. If you're sitting on yours, get up and start using them! The only excuses you have for not doing so are those you create yourself, and if you're that creative, you're equally capable of finding things you could, should, and would like to do.

You're always too young to stop; you're never too old to start. You're *neither*, too young nor too old!

SALE-ING SMOOTHLY INTO MATURITY—OCTOBER 3, 1995

For some, the art of becoming an accomplished and successful entrepreneur is a life long quest, but I've noticed that some neighborhood youngsters begin achieving this status at very young ages, during magazine drive week.

This money raising campaign appears to be the prerogative of the parochial school, or as one of the up and coming sales leaders of tomorrow told us, "The public school kids won't be here, only the Catholic schools do this." This definitive statement was in response to our question about how many of the local neighborhood kids were going to offer us a chance to help them win THE BIG PRIZE!, or even one of the lesser ones being used as incentives to GET OUT AND SELL THOSE MAGAZINES!

We enjoy having the young people come on this annual occasion. The measure of growth from one year to the next is amazing, even though we see them all year long under a variety of circumstances. Socially visiting a neighbor is different than calling on business.

Of course, this transition doesn't occur over night, and a youngster's first sales call in this annual campaign usually takes place before he or she can even read, so an escorting parent or older sibling is a necessity, all of which brings me back to Kevin.

The first year Kevin came on this particular school-related mission, he was accompanied by his oldest brother Todd, who, in fact, did all the work while Kevin sat, squirmed, and softly kept asking, "Are we done yet?"

Two years later Kevin, already a confident second grader, came by himself and even told me about the prizes being offered. I still had to do all the paper work, but he at least knew what forms to keep and what to give me as a receipt. The only disappointment for him was that Mr. Huston wasn't home, but I served as an acceptable substitute since I did order a magazine.

The following day Kevin came again with Kyle, another neighbor boy. There's strength in numbers, (even numbers of two), so Kevin's confidence was buoyed even further as they came in with their order forms for yet *another* sale. This time, Mr. Huston was home. (Same game, new player, different positions.) I returned to the bench on the sidelines.

"Do you have any cookies?" he asked me as my husband leafed through the catalog. I apologized and said I didn't have one single cookie in the house.

There was some further male conversation about model building and magazine choices as well as which boy was going to get credit for this sale, and could they shoot darts. We passed on the darts and concentrated, temporarily, on the magazines.

"You always *used* to have cookies." He was right, of course, but some things have gradually changed around here, like waistlines—a hard concept to explain to a growing boy.

The debate continued among the three of them, with Kevin's strongly suggesting that the solution to the credit issue would be for us to buy two magazines, one from each of them. He even went so far as to offer a suggestion he considered appealing (to *him*).

In response to my husband's joking comment about not being able to understand his choice, Kevin quickly fired back, "It comes with a parent's guide!" Experience is teaching him well. The budding entrepreneur was prepared to deal with almost any obstacles thrown in his path—except my lack of cookies.

As my husband filled out the paper work, Kevin gave it one more try. "Don't you have anything that resembles a cookie?" I really felt bad. I tried to explain that Mr. Huston wasn't supposed to eat cookies so I didn't keep them around as I used to. A kid only understands not being allowed to eat cookies when it's a punishment!

There was some continued conversation about guy things, then an incoming phone call took my husband's attention and ended the visit.

Watching young people develop is such an exciting adventure. It happens so fast, and even though I realize it's happening, I don't always pay close attention. Then suddenly, I'm surprised to hear unfamiliar voices using extensive adult vocabulary with such ease and understanding.

Kevin's oldest brother Todd is now a young adult, working and earning academic recognition in college. His other brother Greg, now in high school, has grown both physically and mentally into a tall, well-developed young man with a very witty, charismatic personality. And Kevin, once regarded as the baby, is growing and maturing.

To think that at the age of three, this child innocently asked me if I was an old lady.

Today he doesn't ask questions like that. He already knows *those* answers. But Kevin still asks me to buy magazines . . . and why I don't have cookies for him!

A Big Lesson From a Little Boy—February 1, 1998

It was one of those dreary days when the rain wouldn't stop and the sky looked like it was going to remain a permanently depressing gray, the kind of day that occasionally sends me in search of an escape from the bleakness of my immediate surroundings. I set out for a local store, hoping to find an amusing distraction to alleviate my discontent and boredom.

Almost immediately upon entering, my outlook on the day was uplifted by a child.

I saw the little boy, perhaps five or six years old, patiently standing near the exit waiting for his mother, one of the many shoppers in a long line at a check out counter.

Gradually, the mysterious operation of the automatic doors independently opening and closing with each customer's entrance or exit began to capture his attention, then became fascinating enough to occupy it fully.

At first, he approached the end set of doors slowly and cautiously, between the entering or exiting of store customers, obviously taking great delight in the simple act of being able to make them move just by his presence.

His next gestures were more experimental: waving an arm in different patterns, sticking one leg out just far enough for the tip of his shoe to activate the signal, casually strolling back and forth in front of them, bobbing up and down as he did so—he was quite pleased with his talent.

After a few more successful tests, his actions became a bit more bold and aggressive. Completely unaware that others might be observing his performance, he assumed the posture of an aspiring David Copperfield, waving an invisible wand to make the doors comply with his commands.

Clearly, he was getting into his routine and taking great pleasure in the results he was producing.

Perhaps the most refreshing aspect of the few minutes I watched him was how easily and innocently he could amuse himself.

He had found a bit of wonderment in an object most of us obliviously pass through, and combined it with generous doses of imagination as he performed "feats of magic" with the wave of his hand, literally. The barely audible verbal commands he ultimately began issuing to the doors were embellishments to the hand gestures, as he enjoyed instant results and momentary power.

Following so closely on the heels of the advertising blitz encouraging parents and grandparents to buy every new toy on the market, or to rush out in search of limited numbers of collectors' items, in a time when some of us wonder if youngsters ever invent their own entertainment instead of relying on television or organized activities to amuse them, it was delightful to witness first-hand how healthy fun was still being self-crafted and free rather than manufactured and boxed for "a *mere* $79.95."

The little boy was engaged in an activity that required no assembly, needed no batteries, and did not send eager-to-please parents off on futile shopping missions.

He could not have read about it in a catalog, discovered it on a shelf in a toy department, admired it in the hands of playmates, or seen it in a television commercial convincing youngsters they won't be fulfilled until they acquire "the entire collection."

He had no need to plead with his parents to buy it for him. It was a nothing, and he had made it into a something.

I was thoroughly entertained by the scene being played out before me, but I felt a twinge of embarrassment knowing I had set out to do exactly what I often accuse so many young people of doing—seek amusement and diversion from without instead of drawing upon my own resources from within.

It also reminded me of how carelessly I'd let all the holiday hype lead me into making broad generalizations about all youngsters. I was so grateful to have my unfair impressions corrected in such a gentle and delightful manner.

By sheer coincidence, I'd ventured out and been treated to something far more gratifying than I could have hoped for—seeing the uncompromised use of a fertile, developing mind in action.

I'd gone out seeking a diversion; a little boy unaware of my presence provided it, but he also brought me back to reality in the process. Curiously, I wondered what innovative amusement he would create next, following one already successful performance on such a bleak day.

I really believe the sky was a bit brighter as I turned around, passed through those "magic doors," and went back home.

A PLACE FOR EVERYTHING—IN MY PURSE
—JUNE 1, 1997

I opened a new box of tea bags and found a complimentary sample packet of four soothing throat lozenges, one each: golden herbal blend, honey-lemon chamomile, harvest cherry, and herbal orange spice. I gave it a perfunctory "hmm," then dropped it into my purse.

The mail arrived and with it came an advertisement containing two samples each of cold/headache/flu tablets. It got the "hmm" then joined the throat lozenges in my purse.

We finished dinner at a rib restaurant, cleaned up as presentably as possible with the little moist towelettes, then noticed there were some unused extras on the table. I "hmmed" briefly, then popped them into my purse.

I unwrapped my after dinner mint as we walked to the car and, not wanting to be a litterbug, stuffed the paper into my purse.

I probably could continue with similar examples of how I've come to house a very strange collection of nonessential items in my purse, but I think you've figured out by now that its function has been expanded way beyond its original purpose. Right off the top of my head I'd say the breakdown of the contents in my purse is in the area of twenty-five percent necessary, seventy-five percent junk!

This is not an example of a place for everything and everything in its place. Most of the stuff in my purse has no place being there. I've developed the lazy habit of using it as a catchall, and seldom ever clean it out.

Little isolated items are the ones that contribute most to this bad habit. There is no easy answer to where

I put one last breath mint from the roll, a stray paper clip I want to keep handy, or the wrapped wad of chewing gum I can't properly dispose of immediately, so I toss it into my purse. That's how my purse came to be the designated holding place for this odd assortment of almost useless items.

My friend Ruth's purse has departments (as opposed to compartments) for cosmetics, produce, kitchenwares, finances, pharmacy needs, photographic equipment, postal and stationery in that suitcase-like purse. She has converted her bag into a portable storage unit for almost anything that might be necessary when she's away from home.

My purse, on the other hand, houses relatively few essentials that I might need away from home. It is the home for orphaned items that have no other place to call their own.

And disposing of them, as in throwing away, is not always an option, except in the case of candy wrappers, if I remember they are in there. For anything else, it is wasteful, sinful, and as soon as it's gone, I know I'll need it. This presumes I will remember having relegated it to the cavernous, cluttered depths of that always available purse, an idea which in itself is laughable.

This wouldn't be so bad if I routinely removed and/or used some of these things. Unfortunately, the motley collection just continues to grow.

Old shopping lists that still have one or two unpurchased items are buried somewhere in there. If my memory serves me correctly (and if the paper hasn't disintegrated), there are window measurements from our previous house written on the back of one of those shopping lists.

I continually open new rolls of mints, take one, then toss the remainder into the purse, easier than trying to find a stray one(s) buried in the lowest level of that bag.

The same is true with tissues. I never assume I'll be able to find anything usable, even though I always add clean ones to the bag before leaving home.

And, may God rest her soul, I still carry my mother's address and phone number, in case of emergency. I probably should find and remove them—I can almost hear her telling me they've been changed.

My purse has a mysterious appeal. Once in awhile, when I have to wait (at an airport, in the doctor's office), I spend a few minutes searching the depths to see what forgotten treasures still exist. It's short-lived entertainment and, upon occasion, has turned up items I no longer recognize.

I don't know what the shelf life of tea bags, painkillers, and throat lozenges is, but I doubt if it really matters much. The likelihood of my finding and using them is only slightly better than my winning the lottery. I'm not overly fond of chamomile, anyway.

A friend who knows me well gave me a large tote bag I probably should carry instead of a purse. In bold black letters it announces: DUMB THINGS I GOTTA CARRY.

In a pathetic sort of way, those five words sum up the contents of my purse.

DON'T DO DUMB THINGS—SEPTEMBER 9, 1995

It is impossible to go through life without some embarrassing incidents. I wish it were otherwise, but reality prohibits me, or anyone else, from enjoying a luxury which simply does not exist.

As long as humans have attempted to communicate with each other, young people have listened one way or another as those older and wiser have issued warnings and advised them to take precautions. Regardless of what specific words were used, or in what language they were delivered, the basic message translates to, "Don't do dumb things!"

It would be more fair if the word "intentionally" were added to those words of wisdom. However, it usually isn't, so if you do something dumb, intentionally or otherwise, count on having someone notice.

A case in point: one morning my husband waved to a neighbor driving down the road with his rubbish cans propped in the open trunk of his car. After he waved, the neighbor apparently glanced in his rear view mirror, saw the open trunk, and realized what he had done. He returned and deposited the cans at the end of his driveway where they belonged for pick up.

He resumed his trip into town, waving and smiling at my husband, again, this time with a shrug and a slightly embarrassed expression that merely said, "What can I say, it's Monday morning!"

The rubbish can tale reminded me of yet another vehicle story from many years ago. Our son was out working in the yard when a different neighbor drove by and waved—we lived on a friendly road. Our son waved back, then began waving with a great deal more enthusiasm, but received no immediate reaction.

Several months later, when we gathered for a neighborhood picnic, our son asked this person if his radio survived the trip on the trunk of his car. After looks of open-mouthed amazement, we heard the whole story.

Our son had been trying to call the neighbor's attention to a radio resting on the trunk of the car; our neighbor thought we had the friendliest kid on the road. The radio, presumably misplaced by the "kids who don't take care of anything!" had, for awhile, been a minor bone of contention in the family.

After explanations took his kids off the hook, our neighbor finally realized he owed them a long overdue apology, a position no one enjoys. Sheepishly, but sincerely, Dad apologized and everyone, including his kids, laughed for a long time over the *really* portable radio!

I think one of the greatest gifts is being able to regard a mishap or misunderstanding in a humorous way, rather than always first assuming it is either an ominous message or the ultimate example of permanently loosing face.

Really serious problems cannot be laughed off lightly, and in no way do I mean to confuse them with life's little embarrassing moments. As long as I correctly distinguish between the two, I just try to remember to use my handy *faux pas* license, which allows me to laugh at myself as well as reinterpret the French term into meaning "temporary egg on the face," with the emphasis on temporary.

Embarrassing moments are strangers to no one. My friend Pauline won't mind my telling you about her phone call to me. She had been through a dreadful series of health problems that had kept her house bound and immobilized for months. During her recovery period, she was limited to reading, watching television, then, after a time, talking briefly on the phone.

Her red-faced moment came when she entered my entire phone number, then wondered why she didn't hear any ringing. How she laughed at herself when she discovered she was holding her television remote control up to her ear!

Since life without some embarrassment is outside the realm of reality, the next best alternative for me is to at least try to avoid as many uncomfortable circumstances as possible, deal with those that are unavoidable as well as I can, and at all times remember, either way, they provide fodder when I need an amusing anecdote to lighten my day.

So if I occasionally leave leftovers in the refrigerator long enough to decompose, I look at them as compost for the garden. If I put potatoes into the oven to cook without turning on the heat, it does not indicate my memory is deserting me. It means instead of lamenting over a lousy dinner, we go out to eat.

Face it. Unless I leave the planet, I'm going to wind up with my share of embarrassing moments. And even though I sometimes think I'm also getting someone else's share as well, I know that feeling will pass.

The important thing is to remember the original advice: Try not to do dumb things, but for those times when you do, keep your *faux pas* licenses handy. They're free, available to anyone and, they never expire!

Some Scents Make No Sense—July 8, 1997

The cologne a woman wears makes a statement about her. Some choose that fragrance with ease. I, on the other hand, find it a mind-boggling challenge. I hear its name and my nose goes into denial.

I at least knew what to expect when perfumes had familiar names with matching aromas like Lilac or Gardenia.

Today's offerings—Obsession?—Poison?—appear obliquely mysterious and more threatening-sounding than attractive. They conjure up visions of wicked stepmothers brewing vile-smelling concoctions and plotting evil deeds with a talking mirror. They don't rate a whiff of consideration.

Even worse than wicked stepmothers is the disturbing thought of smelling like a wet ox, the repugnant image the musk colognes bring to my mind. They may be quite pleasant, but I'll never know.

Although my rational mind knows better, it nevertheless rejects anything called *toilet water*, or *eau de toilette*, if you prefer. Just imagining a porcelain chamber pot (in *any* language) as the source of one's fragrance is totally unappealing.

I had no ideas colors smelled—White Shoulders, White Linen, Red. I might try Red, only because I like the color, hardly a sensible way to select a fragrance.

To hurdle this obstacle, I used to ask my husband for his opinion. After he once said (nicely) what I had on smelled like insect repellent, I decided I didn't need that much honesty!

To my knowledge, there are no rules stating we must smell like flowers, animals, colors, or chamber pots. Therefore, I'd like to resort to something I do understand when I select a cologne—the aromas of foods.

Entering a kitchen with the lingering aroma of freshly baked bread, cookies, or pie is a euphoric experience. The appealing, spicy smell of warm gingerbread makes me feel good, and that's the statement I want to make: *I feel good!*

I believe I could successfully start a whole new trend with my own line, "The Kitchen Cupboard Collection." Little dabs of anise or vanilla for a sweet accent, a light dusting of cinnamon or nutmeg for a headier appeal. Hot apple pie for daytime wear, and chocolate anything for anytime.

Surely others who share this selection problem would welcome this sensible approach to choosing scents. One woman I know who *loves* garlic has already said she'd wear it in a heartbeat.

When this catches on, I'll suggest to her, (as a friend, naturally), that the amount she wears should not equal what she uses in cooking. New trends, after all, should be discriminating and this is about making statements, not enemies!

BUGS ASSUME RIGHT OF EMINENT DOMAIN
—JULY 16, 1994

There are pros and cons to living out in the country that involve more than the amount of work required to maintain a place with acreage. Usually, the pros win, barely, but some days my tolerance is sorely tested.

I can tolerate the rabbits who daintily nibble the tender buds from every plant. I'm a sucker for those soft, twitching noses.

I usually manage to ignore the nightly screeches of raccoons fighting amongst themselves over food, even though they resemble an old, badly scratched Rudee Vallee recording played at the wrong speed. I do not, however, appreciate the orchestral accompaniment as they tip trash cans.

I forgive (most of the time) the chipmunks who either trample the flowers, or tunnel under and force the young plants right out of the ground. I even overlook their noisy excursions in and out of the drain pipes. I admire the speed and agility of Chip, Dale, and all their relatives.

I alternately curse and feel pity for skunks. Most people move to the country to enjoy the fresh air, but these little creatures frequently pollute it out of self defense. Necessary, effective, but definitely unpleasant.

I try not to sound too much like a shrew when the squirrels skitter across the porch, then up into the tree, from whence they throw down pine cones and scold me. Actually, it's a bit disconcerting when I realize that I'm arguing back—and they always get in the last word.

I watch, properly subordinate, when the woodchucks strut around as though they hold the mortgage papers on the place. They exercise their rights to wander at will, gorge themselves constantly on anything we try to grow, and redesign the landscape to suit their needs.

I even force myself to stop comparing the frequent, raucous gatherings of black birds out on the lawn to scenes from an Alfred Hitchcock movie.

BUT, I cannot tolerate the creeping, crawling, flying, buzzing, stinging, biting bugs!

It isn't that I dislike or dismiss the need for bugs in the overall balance of nature, but I have strong feelings about fairness and sharing. There's plenty of room and I'm willing to coexist with (almost) all creatures. But this has become a one-way proposition—*their* way!

All I want is to remain unstung, unbitten, and uncrawled on when I sit outside on the swing. That seems like such a small request when I think of how much free reign the creatures already have. Desperately wanting to isolate and preserve my little bug-free space has led me to try some usual measures to discourage insect invasions.

We've used bug repellents guaranteed to protect an area the size of Rhode Island. Right! We've had bug zappers that would make Crankshaft's look like a fading pocket flashlight!

A citronella candle protects the one person who hovers dangerously close to the flame, unless you light enough of them to build a pep rally-sized bonfire. Then, of course, you have to deal with constant waves of nausea.

I've even smeared potions on my exposed skin. Along with the fact that they stink, the creepy, crawly critters have built up immunities to the very chemical weapons that are supposed to be such a threat to them. We humans should have such adaptive abilities!

Studies have shown these pests are attracted by any scents we apply daily anyway, so I'll be doggoned if I'm going to abandon the use of deodorant, soap, and shampoo just because some bug gets turned on! Hey, they're indifferent to whether the scent is pleasant or putrid. Surely you've noticed insects are just as prevalent when you're working up a good, grimy sweat doing yard work. They have no taste, so it's difficult to fake them out.

Not only are they pervasive, but they engage in sneaky tactics. The smaller they are, the greater the challenge. They land, have an appetizer, entree, dessert, and then leave, all before I frantically swat the swelling bumps they've left as payment. By then they've moved elsewhere for after dinner drinks. Sometimes I feel as though my body is hosting several progressive dinners at the same time!

This is not a symbiotic relationship! I don't engage in activities with anything that has more legs or eyes than I have. The fact that I shouldn't pick on anything that isn't at least my own size has no bearing, either. I may be bigger, but they're *smarter*.

This is developing into all out warfare and I'm losing. I can't even claim small victories. How can such small "things" continuously manage to be so outwitting?

I propose they grant me a tiny space outdoors that

would be off limits to them. I want to strike a bargain with them that will allow me the undisturbed use of my swing for certain periods of the day or evening in exchange for their roaming freely everywhere else. I want them to stop thinking of my body as their Perle Mesta place for socializing. Is that too much to ask?

Something tells me I'd probably have more success wishing for Camelot or finding Brigadoon!

SHOPPING: A LITTLE TRIP OF HORRORS
—DECEMBER 2, 1993

I normally do not have the personality of the Grinch who stole Christmas. However, every December I qualify for the title. Every holiday season, I coach myself about handling "the dreaded task" as an adult instead of with resistance. I've tried for years, but I am still balking!

I enjoy almost everything else about Christmas But. . . *I do not like to shop!* When I have to get serious about this task I experience cold sweats, light headedness, and downright adamant stubbornness about even entering a store.

I can hear some women gasping in shock, whispering behind cupped hands, pointing accusing fingers. Talk about odd! Whoever heard of a woman who didn't like to shop?!

I came equipped with all the necessary genes to verify my female status except for that shopping thing. Nothing in me wants to "shop-'til-I-drop." I "stall-outside-the-mall!" I can rattle off a dozen excuses to avoid shopping, and if they fail, I have ten more on standby.

I really love giving gifts. If I could buy them without burrowing through all mankind (personkind?), the holidays might be perfect. And a catalog is not a viable solution—that's like trying to make a recipe look as appealing as its picture in an ad. No, I have no choice but to face reality and enter the lion's den known as *the mall.*

Crowds overwhelm me. I lose my concentration jockeying for position in stores. I lose the only item in the necessary size because I am intimidated by defiant "don't-even-think-about-it" looks. I lose my already pathetic sense of direction, repeatedly turning the wrong way as I exit stores. If he's with me, I lose my husband as my numbed body naturally gravitates in any direction with fewer people. I lose my car because I can't remember where I parked it, or for that matter, which door I entered. I lose my courage when I have to guess at what might appeal to those on my list. I even lose my list! Let's face it, in the shopping world, I'm the born loser!

I envy women who enthusiastically recount their dawn-to-dusk shopping excursions. Their excitement grows as they detail each valuable find. Friendly competition heats up as they vie for best bargain of the day. It's the shopper's version of "the thrill of victory, the agony of defeat," and true shoppers do not go down to defeat without a good fight! I shudder and break out in a cold sweat just listening.

When Christmas gets frighteningly close and I have stalled, procrastinated, and am running out of both excuses and time, I usually force myself to enter the arena, unarmed, unwilling, and often unsuccessful. Surely there are better alternatives. I've even wrapped up pictures cut from magazines. (I know, tacky!)

In desperate moments, I've seriously considered applying to become an apprentice to the Grinch. I'd be a Grinch*ette*, or a Grinch*esse*. Perhaps I'd even qualify to win an award as "Grinch of the Month." Then I'd be honor bound to avoid shopping, legitimately. After all, no self-respecting Grinch would be caught shopping, in a mall or anywhere else. I can handle that!

No Pets Among Peeves—June 24, 1997

As time goes by I'm discovering my list of pet peeves is expanding and becoming quite long.

For example, on one of my infrequent but necessary shopping forays, I asked a salesman a simple question, what he considered his best vacuum cleaner. His reply began, "At your age. . . ." Any chance of his making a sale was gone!

I have no problem with my age, but total strangers who assume that having gray hair means being physically and mentally challenged annoy me. The man knew nothing about me, yet concluded I was probably weak, feeble, and in need of assistance. I wanted information about a machine, not his misguided, inaccurate concepts about the person buying it.

Another pet peeve of mine is the automobile sales person who repeatedly asks the inane question, "What do we have to do to put you in this car today?" We once dealt with a salesman who said that so often (between trips to conspire with his manager during the negotiations), I vowed never to set foot in that dealership again.

Still another is hearing someone say to a retiree, "What on earth do you do with all your free time?" This is one more of those absurd conclusions drawn by those who assume that retiring is synonymous with rotting. I don't know who plants these misbegotten notions but there are a great many of them in circulation.

Most of my peeves deal with dumb statements I hear, but are not limited to just that.

There was a time when a tag on a mattress or cushion warning me not to remove it under penalty of law intimidated me. It also annoyed me because I didn't know why it was prohibited. Would all the stuffing disappear if the tag was gone? What kind of law protects pillows and mattresses, and who decided they need protection anyway?

I finally decided to defy the stupid warning and risk the penalty, whatever it was. I cut off every tag I could find. The stuffing remained intact, and the tag police didn't come to arrest me. The warning still exists, and I still don't know what the penalty is, but I'm no longer intimidated by it.

Although I do it all the time, it really makes no sense to use the words "pet" and "peeve" in the same phrase. "Pet" usually suggests something favorite, while "peeve" implies a complaint. If so, does that make a *pet peeve* a favorite complaint? Does that qualify as an oxymoron, or just moronic?

Whatever they're called, and regardless of whether I hear or see them, they exist. In talking with others I've learned most people have their own lists of pet peeves, and, not surprising, share many of the same ones with others.

My friend Joanna and I both react to the aggravating speech habit of leaving the letters *"ed"* off the ends of certain words. In some of the more common examples, the guilty person uses whip cream instead of whipp*ed* cream, eats cream chip beef rather than cream*ed* chipp*ed* beef, and refers to old fashion things, not old fashion*ed* things . . . Damn*ed* if I can figure out why!

When I was a kid, my mother would tell me to save the dishes after drying them. Save? It was years before

I learned other people put away their dishes. It was frustrating, but I never did convince her to stop "saving" them. I certainly tried for years, as much to her chagrin, I'm sure, as mine.

The commonly used expression "Save it for good" was (and still is) equally irksome. When I got new clothing for Christmas or a birthday, I had to wait for a special occasion to wear it. You know, as a kid, you risk outgrowing clothing before getting to wear it when you have to operate on that premise. Again, it was years before I understood why clothing always was purchased so many sizes too big. The word "save" had to be directly related to the Depression.

A pet peeve our daughter shares with many people is the driver who's never learned how to use the little stick on the left side of the steering column, that individual who apparently believes if he's turning or changing lanes, everyone will know and give him the needed space. Interesting, he's usually mastered horn-beeping. Go figure.

As difficult as it is not to do so, reacting negatively to pet peeves is usually futile. The wiser, and surely more mature, action would be to try to ignore them. Most offenders rarely realize the effects they have on others, and it's unrealistic to think we can, or even should be able to, change behaviors in others.

As contradictory as it is, however, I still catch myself using the words "pet" and "peeve" in that commonly accepted phrase, "pet peeve." Apparently, I've elevated the status of complaining to an acceptable skill by singling out and constantly focusing on my own favorites.

You say you, too, have mastered the art of complaining? You'd like to receive the recognition coming to you for this accomplishment? Get in line behind me, please; I have a pet peeve about spongers, too.

I believe I've just complained my way to the head of the line.

All For One And One For All—December 28,1995

Who is this mysterious person named All? You've no doubt seen the name. Popular designers and clothing manufacturers like B.U.M., Bugle Boy, and Gitano are vying to merge and produce clothes for her on a grand scale.

Many clothing manufacturers are going into business with this faceless individual. Just check the tags on some garments being sold: "One Size Fits All", or, as it's becoming familiarly known, "1SFA". Again I ask, who is *All*?

Obviously, this All isn't humanly capable of inflating and deflating at will, which would then, and only then, give credibility to the advertised statement. Therefore, her garments have to be designed so that regardless of who puts them on, they will "fit." She must be the "creation" of a designer who has given status to wearing belted bed sheets.

Normally the word *fit* implies that at specific points the configuration of the clothing corresponds to some degree with the contours of a person's body. However, there are no rules that state the corresponding configurations have to be the same for all people. Hence, one size does fit all, "fit" being determined totally by the individual.

If there really were any truth in advertising, the tags would have to read "1SFN": One Size Fits Nobody, but being classified as a nobody certainly would put a crimp on sales. This is surely a case of being a somebody, part of a group, even if it means wearing something large enough to cover the entire group at the same time.

It simply might be that physical freedom is the overriding appeal of wearing a garment in which it is possible to get lost. Even in the most personally tailored clothing, there are restrictions that hamper or restrain us.

Then again, this may be an attempt to recreate the feelings we had as young children, when the word style was not yet a part of our vocabulary. Conscientious parents considered warmth, durability, and economics when determining what we wore, criteria that often had absolutely nothing to do with fashion.

I know as a young child the importance of my clothing was measured by how freely I was able to run, jump, and move about. Maybe some of us don't always want to be grown up. This would certainly be one way to make that statement.

Sometimes it's difficult to believe women will confidently appear in public wearing an article of clothing they think is attractive when in truth it is simply designed to cover the body. This may be one reason why the astute members of the design world have been able to capitalize on this feature and make it trendy. Omar, the Tent Maker is nobody's fool. He has us all beating down the flaps of his tent in order to remain stylish and comfortable.

I still like clothing that allows some freedom of movement. A roomy sweatshirt is just about the most comfortable item of clothing I own, so I understand a little why loose, unrestricted garments hold appeal. There is one aspect of this fashion statement I can't quite get through my head, though.

The extreme of this particular style includes a big, floppy shirt that would hang down to my knees, with

the shoulder seam half way down my upper arm, a neck-
line large enough to fit my waist, and the main body
wide enough to accommodate Michael Dean Perry. . . and
it's often worn over stretch pants that are so close-fitting
there's legitimate concern about cutting off circulation!
These two items are often sold as an outfit, and both have
1SFA tags on them.

Should we assume from this combination that the
creator of All's wardrobe is enjoying some amusement
at our expense? Does this designer, in fact, picture All
as having spindly legs like Olive Oyl with the upper body
of a Sumo wrestler?

In truth, I have next to no interest in constantly
changing styles and fads. I can't even pronounce the
names of most designers. The fashion industry has always
been a enigma to me, and a recent article from Paris
previewing the coming spring styles merely reinforced
my confusion.

The headlines touted colors ranging from "beaming
pastels to shimmering sherbets and pulsating pop
colors," yet the largest photograph featured a model in
a black satin Claude Montana ensemble. Her oddly
organized red hair lent the only color to an outfit
described as having feather-like details. Truth: she
looked like a turkey in a tuxedo.

Naturally, Claude wouldn't appreciate my description, but then, I wouldn't wear his creation, either, and
I can honestly say I don't know anyone else who would,
even on Halloween. Is there licorice sherbet? . . . With
feathers?

Perhaps this unknown person All, of 1SFA fame, and
for whom so many manufacturers are now designing
clothing, does make the sensible fashion statement to a
majority of the people after all. Even if it doesn't match

all the parts of a person's body, it is recognized as "real people clothing."

I think All is beginning to take on the appearance of someone I know, and she wasn't among the models from the Paris show. I strongly suspect All lives in my neighborhood, in my home. . . .

Son of a gun, I think All lives on the other side of my mirror!

MELONS, MATES, AND OTHER IMPORTANT PICKS
——JUNE 30, 1994

Next time you have an opportunity to do so, try casually lingering in the produce department of a large supermarket on a busy day. It would be worth the price of an admission ticket to observe the various ways in which shoppers make their selections.

For example, choosing a head of lettuce apparently requires a unique skill. Probably everyone asked would offer a different opinion on what is the proper technique, but I'm fascinated by all of them. Also, I've learned if I can give the impression of attending to the same details as a nearby selective and fussy shopper long enough, I can get what would have been the second choice of this seemingly knowledgeable person. I'll be honest here, she gives the matter such serious thought and attention she really must know something I don't know about lettuce!

Whether copying others or exercising personal techniques in a quest for quality, shoppers seem to agree gently squeezing, sniffing, tapping, listening to, and shaking the produce will give the desired results. I don't fully understand how these measures are supposed to work, but I continue to practice them.

If a cantaloupe rattles when I shake it, I become suspicious and select another. If it smells like a cantaloupe, I am reassured. My decision to continue the procedure depends on how badly I want melon.

Watermelons pose the greatest challenge to me. The squeezing part is pretty clear: if any part of that large, heavy fruit gives under the pressure of my touch it becomes an instant reject. And smelling anything with such a thick rind would be rather futile, I believe. Besides, there's something undignified about leaning over and sniffing from melon to melon, and I'm not about to lift and shake, so that leaves tapping and listening.

Actually, it's more like thumping my knuckles against the thing, which is kind of silly since I don't know what a good melon sounds like even though several helpful friends have told me what to listen for. All watermelons sound alike to me. The only sure thing I do know is I'm not listening for a response from within!

No matter what I do, I'm convinced the odds of picking a sweet, juicy melon are on a par with rolling dice, maybe I'll win, maybe I won't, but I'll do a lot of guessing and hoping for the best in the process.

Not long ago, one of my produce-picking observations focused on a young couple, possibly newlyweds. I watched them attempting to arrive at a mutual method of produce selection, just one of the many decisions they must learn to make together. I then was struck by the thought that, in a peculiar sort of way, the process of choosing melons and mates could be considered quite similar. I began to wonder how these two people had chosen each other.

How much had each been able to learn about the other just from seeing the outside, particularly when most young adults aren't sure what they're looking for?

I doubted if they'd relied on the same methods used for selecting bananas or tomatoes since those methods aren't even fool proof when picking produce, much less a mate for life.

There had to be a lot of guessing involved after they met, were seeing each other regularly and began weighing the possibility of spending the rest of their lives together. What outward signs offered reassurance that the inside person would be equally as appealing as the outer one?

The squeezing part of trying to find out about each other was probably fun, but they might have had difficulty giving a satisfactory or acceptable explanation for using thumping and shaking as ways of determining suitability. Clearly, figuring out how to properly make choices can create more questions than answers.

In spite of the obstacles, as well as knowing there are only so many things that can be fully checked out ahead of time, most people continue to seek out what they hope will be the perfect mate. Even with so many unanswered questions most of us are still willing to try to find the best, using whatever means we can.

Just as with picking out produce, there is that element of chance, combined with a lot of hope and optimism, that we'll make the best decision possible with the information we have. After observing, listening, discussing, and using any other forms of research available to us, we eventually arrive at the time to make our decision, cross our fingers, and go for it, whether it's a melon or a mate.

Our celebration of another anniversary is pretty strong evidence the man I met in 1950, and married a few years later, proved to be the right choice. Fortunately, we both feel we made the best selections (and it wasn't without a few figurative knuckle thumps along the way).

Now, if I could only pick melons as well!

THE LONGEST DISTANCE BETWEEN TWO POINTS
—JANUARY 2, 1994

To paraphrase a familiar quote, when you're up to your tush in alligators, it's easy to forget the original objective was to drain the swamp. This observation, coupled with the opposing way in which males and females approach various tasks, creates an interesting pattern in our daily routine. We often start with the same goals, but arriving at them is definitely a study in contrasts.

A series of events that occurred one morning shortly before the holidays demonstrates how differently male and female minds can operate. My husband was digging out an old table top from a basement cupboard on which to mount a Christmas tree stand. He knew the detached legs were in the upper garage, so he went to retrieve them.

Once there, the game plan changed considerably. He saw that the waiting Christmas tree was in need of water, which he gave it after he found a hand saw with which to cut off the bottom. He started to rewind the hose for winter storage, but decided this was as good a time as any to do a quick desalting of the cars. With that task out of the way, he detached and wound the hose, swept up the sawdust from the tree, gathered up the saw and some other tools lying near the door, and headed for the lower garage to put everything away.

While in the process of putting away things, he saw the charger under the workbench which, in turn, reminded him he had to remove the batteries from the tractors, charge them, then bring them into the house for the winter. He took them out, cleaned them, and hooked them up to the charger. While they were charging, he detached the mowers and got the plow ready to mount on the tractor, removed the mulcher cover from the hand mower, cleaned up the mess it had left on the floor, and stored it in its rightful place on the wall.

He was hanging the mower parts right next to parts for the old '56 pickup truck, one of the things he was getting ready for our son to work on while he was home for Christmas. As he thought about our son, he remembered he had to get out an old faucet our son needed for his own garage sink. In case our son wanted to cart all those things back to Houston, my husband set them down beside the charger, then noticed it was time to unhook the batteries and take them up to the house.

He passed the woodpile as he walked towards the back door, discovering more wood cutting tools as well as the squirrel trap, all of which also had to be stored. He set the batteries down on the step, put away those particular items, then walked out to pick up the arriving mail.

He came into the house with the mail (and even remembered the batteries—it was either that or trip over them, I guess), gave me the former and took the latter down to store in the basement cupboard.

Lo and behold, there was that table top! The one that needed legs. The legs he originally set out to get much earlier that morning. The legs that were still in the upper garage, right above the tree he watered three hours earlier!

Although taking such a circuitous route is nothing new, I was still curious about what activities had divided his attention this time. If I had just asked him what he'd been doing, he probably would have said he was getting the legs for the table, but since I always forget how one errand can take three hours, he carefully, patiently, and logically explained exactly how one thing had led to another.

To me, it sounded like going from Cleveland to Chicago by way of New York, but his common sense approach explained how a ten minute task could very easily turn into three hours. I'm sure it's that *man thing* I can't understand.

But then, turnabout is fair play. He wouldn't be able to understand how I would have been able to walk past all those other tasks, even if they were "right on the way."

This is an example of how things sometimes happen around here. In the course of setting out to do one job, numerous others inevitably do spring up along the way, and my husband seems to be compelled to attend to all of them immediately. I, on the other hand, can walk right past several tasks if they are not number one on my "to-do" list! Somehow, between us, things do get done around here, but I don't often try to explain how.

Our different approaches are amusing most of the time, but I sincerely hope I'm not with him if he ever sets out to drain a swamp!

WAIT! I MAY HAVE A COUPON—AUGUST 3, 1996

Please say my husband and I aren't alone in turning some simple decisions into totally out of proportion issues. Major decisions often appear easy to resolve, but by comparison, certain seemingly unimportant ones stall us constantly. This oddity can't be unique to just us.

A prime example of this situation occurs when one asks the other if he/she would like to eat out instead of eating at home. Most people welcome that opportunity, but for us, it initiates a familiar dialogue liberally peppered with the operative phrase, "I don't know, what do you want to do?"

So begins the volley of non-opinions in this senseless exchange of words because neither one wants to be in charge, to risk being the one who might make a bad decision. Each is trying to determine what the other wants to do. Even after so many years of marriage, we still play this dumb game.

After sufficiently bantering enough "I don't knows", we eventually get to "It's okay with me, if you want to go," and decide to eat out. Hurdle number one cleared. Next, where to go.

"I don't know, where do you want to go?"

"I don't know, what do you feel like eating?"

"I don't know, it doesn't matter to me."

"Is there anything you don't particularly want to eat?"

When all else fails, we eliminate what we don't want instead of choosing what we do want. It's definitely a "bass-ackwards" system, but it narrows the field. It also wastes so much time that what would have been lunch is now going to be an early dinner. The next question usually contributes to the ultimate decision.

"What do we have coupons for?"

Merchants encourage the public to patronize their establishments by offering reductions with coupons. Not only do these coupons keep the competition active, they help to expedite our belabored process of selection. For us, restaurants offering coupons are often the *main* contenders.

I produce my packet of current bargains, dismiss the ones we've already eliminated for whatever reason, pitch the ones that have expired, and list off what's left. The field is narrowed even further.

Finally, after a few more rounds of "I don't know, what do you want," we reach a decision and head for the restaurant. If you haven't guessed, the next obstacle looms when we have to choose something from a four page menu.

By now so much time has passed almost everything looks good, including foods we normally wouldn't eat. Having a valuable coupon got us to the restaurant; having one that includes almost every entree on the menu has put us back to square one.

"What are you going to have?"

"I don't know, what are you going to order?"

Incidentally, it makes no difference who asks first. We've practiced this go-nowhere routine for so long either of us can do the asking or answering.

By this time serious hunger is beginning to take over, trying to control our minds in much the same way it does when we make the mistake of going grocery shopping with empty stomachs. With enough condiments and side dishes, Charlie Chaplin's boiled shoe would look appetizing.

Understandably, the server's loss of patience becomes thinly veiled after repeated trips to our table still find us stalled over the menu. At times I've considered telling a server to surprise me with anything just to avoid the whole decision-making process.

Just being so indecisive in this situation isn't bad enough. My conscience compounds the problem, reminding me other people may be waiting for the table we're occupying, hungry diners who probably already know what they want to eat. When there are no other guests waiting to be seated, I suspect I've delayed for so long it's nearly closing time.

Even if it has to be done with the "jab-a-finger-at-the-menu-with-closed-eyes" method, we eventually order and eat our meals. Surprisingly, we usually enjoy it but eating that late at night makes sleeping difficult.

We often go through this inane process when I can't think of something interesting or different to cook for dinner, a dilemma that is becoming more and more frequent. I'm fully aware of our track record, so even I find it hard to believe I do this, but I'll ask my husband what he'd like for dinner and predictably, he says, "I don't know, what do you want?" No surprises there.

This goes on for a few minutes until we come full circle and one says, "Would you just like to go out to eat?"

"I don't know, would *you?*"

"Oh, I don't know . . . Where would *you* like to go?"

Have coupon, we'll eat out.

If restaurants ever stop offering coupon specials, we're gonna starve!

IT'S WAR BETWEEN MAN AND SQUIRREL
—AUGUST 1, 1997

Blending different personalities to resolve issues in relationships is an ongoing adventure. Until you've become fully entrenched in this activity, you can't begin to understand how this necessary process works.

One example is the serious quest to outwit a squirrel. In the warfare my husband wages against this pesky rodent who repeatedly invades the bird feeders I am a witness, not a participant. I support, applaud, and appreciate his efforts. Occasionally, however, I laugh.

The battle between man and beast is not new. It has raged for many years, but only after we had a yard of our own (or what we thought was our own), did we become involved in this particular fray.

I once believed Mother Nature maintained a balance of fair living standards among her progeny. Eventually I accepted the standards were neither balanced nor fair and stopped interfering in the struggle to make them so, but the male need to declare territorial rights persisted.

Let me tell you right up front, a squirrel *always* wins!

This conflict is not unique, and my husband is not alone in his attempts to safeguard the food he provides for the birds against invaders. Almost to a man, literally, the husbands among most of our friends are similarly engaged in squirrel skirmishes. These mighty warriors have thoroughly discussed and debated the topic of "them against us."

They all have done extensive research and compared techniques; shared non-lethal weapons (don't alert the animal rights activists, please, they use only "have-a-heart' traps"); collaborated on the merits of various creative strategies; even rated the success of maneuvers on a scale of one to three (they can't go higher, nothing is ever totally successful). Unfortunately, the results they can share: squirrels, victorious—humans, frustrated.

What I once thought of as a cute little bright-eyed, bushy-tailed woodland creature has been transformed into an evil-eyed, devious menace who is smarter than the average human. He (and I suspect this may be a male versus male challenge) possesses many of the qualities needed to be victorious: resourcefulness, guile, uncanniness, stamina, and diligence. Unlike his human counterparts, however, he has no conscience and follows no rules.

Throughout this never-ending confrontation my husband, who has the same admirable characteristics but is governed by his conscience and a need to abide by rules, has resorted to some near-extreme measures in defense of the birds' food.

He placed the feeders as far from trees as possible to discourage airborne invasions from nearby branches. Flying squirrel is not an expression to be taken lightly.

He contrived over-sized, slanted, cone-shaped metal hoods to cover the freestanding feeders. Challenging, but still negotiable landing fields for incoming flights.

He devised shields using extra large garbage can lids to protect against assaults from the bottom. They are orange barrels to the squirrel, posing temporary detours or inconvenience, but nothing more.

He even greased the metal pole holding the feeders. As hilarious as it was to watch, the struggle to scale the pole ceased to be amusing when the squirrel's diligence (climb and slip, climb and slip), finally rewarded him— the grease wore off. Once again victory was his in the struggle for territorial rights and dominance.

Along with his other qualities, a squirrel also exhibits enviable athletic prowess and unflagging stamina. Because of these additional, advantageous attributes, he broad jumps like Carl Lewis, vertical jumps like Michael Jordon, and runs like Michael Johnson.

The uncanny squirrel manages to stay one step ahead of his opponent with Patton-like ingenuity, strategy, and tenacity. He thoroughly frustrates his human male enemy, eventually engaging him in comical shouting matches.

Now, there's a sight to behold, an adult man of a higher order of intelligence, shouting imprecations at a "dumb" animal perched high up in a tree. The squirrel's chattering is really laughter. The more recognizable laughter is mine.

But his insult of insults is walking, *walking*, right past the baited trap as the human watches from a window. I'm not sure, but I think I've seen him thumb his nose. Honest!

Nevertheless, the human continues to fight back, trying in vain to outwit the cagey animal, knowing full well as he attempts to counter one assault, the resourceful little squirrel is already devising a new foil. If that squirrel weren't so annoying, I could respect his fortitude.

Don't be misled by that adorable, chubby-cheeked little face. Look again at that expression. It's saying, "Gotcha!"

My husband is becoming a battle-weary combatant against the guile of a squirrel. I tease him about his lion-hunt tactics to outwit a small rodent, but still he persists, in spite of constant defeat by the crafty squirrel and good-natured mockery by me.

Is it possible the reason these men can't dominate in this war is because the squirrels they're trying so hard to outwit are . . . female?

A THOUSAND PICTURES—A SINGLE WORD
—FEBRUARY 3, 1996

I have about a thousand pictures I usually describe with just one word: unseen!

In the early years of our children's lives, we took a lot of pictures, beautiful, colorful slides that looked simply magnificent when displayed on a large, fold-up screen. I rapidly learned to dislike them!

Originally, I was in favor of this means of preserving our family on film. That was before I realized I would never have a purse full of photographs I could produce with the slightest provocation, or with no provocation. All my friends were showing off their progeny while ours were captured, literally, on tiny cardboard-bound squares of film in a carousel—in a box—on a shelf—gathering dust. I developed a contemptuous attitude towards slides.

It was, and still is, easier to corner people for three minutes at work, in a restaurant, or in a moving car to share your latest photos. They had no choice but to look at them and ooh properly since there was no immediate escape route available to them, and, frankly, three minutes was a small price to pay for when their next rolls of film would be developed. Turnabout is fair play.

On the other hand, coercing invited guests to spend the time while visiting in your home viewing an 80-slide carousel gave them the feeling of being held captive and definitely knocked you out of the running for hostess of the year. It became a production to which even I opposed being subjected. My negative feelings about slides continued to intensify. Before long, our slide-taking sessions went the same way as our home movies.

Yes, we also had an eight-millimeter movie camera with which we tried to preserve our family in action. Our attempts with it were even more short-lived. The technology still was relatively new so the "actors" moved like Charlie Chaplin's Tramp. We have so many boring film-feet of people waddling and waving. Alert friends and family soon learned to wave farewell before the camera appeared.

Our home movies were put to rest on the shelf even faster than the slides. Fortunately for them, our kids grew up and escaped before we had a chance to experiment with video cameras. They were often too busy to stop for prolonged picture-taking sessions, so we finally accepted the futility of our methods.

We managed to snap them trimming the Christmas tree which was good. We have a wonderful record of their physical growth as measured by each year's tree, and eventually we did remember to have regular "non-slide" film in the camera for this annual event. At these times, and only at these times, were my words about cameras and photographs positive.

There was that time after we'd become empty-nesters when I thought it would be so nice to put together an album for each of our children, a visual memento, a step-by-step pictorial journey of their growing years.

Obviously, it couldn't be done with slides, unless I was willing to spend a king's ransom having hundreds of them made into photographs. While many people undertake this project, I decided the cost was too prohibitive. Once again I found myself cursing those stupid slides.

A moment of nostalgia prompted us one cold day to resurrect some of the old home movies, if for no other reason but to amuse, perhaps even embarrass, our children. We carted out all the equipment, set up the screen, threaded the old projector, turned it on, and the bulb burned out.

It definitely put the day's viewing on hold, but the real set back came when we discovered the price of a new bulb for our antiquated movie projector nearly exceeded the original cost of the camera and projector combined.

Somewhere in all this activity there had been the germ of an idea. Besides the amusement factor, we thought we might be able to sort through our pictures and come up with a selection we could transfer to a video tape. The idea seemed to have some merit, especially since the photo album failed. In the process, I also might have been motivated to learn how to operate the VCR. Neither goal was accomplished.

But even if I had succeeded in that mission, our visual, chronological diary would have been considered obsolete before we viewed it. As of today, anyway, pictorially recording somehow incorporates a computer, which only complicates my dilemma further.

It may be easy enough for a child to operate, but as far as I'm concerned, they're the only ones capable of easily manipulating these machines. All this merely caused me to decry photographic technology that much more.

I remain picture poor, unless old school pictures count, but it's embarrassing trying to explain why our thirty-something offspring look so young.

Yes, I have thousands of pictures that can be described with one word. Publicly, the word is "unseen." However, privately that word loosely translates to: #@!&*%#@!

He Says! ... She thinks ... They Know!
—DECEMBER 18, 1992

Photo technology is my personal enigma. Other forms of mechanical "things" I leave to my husband. For example, one morning a strange sound emanating from the water softener prompted both of us to think the day was about to become less than auspicious, but I didn't have to deal directly with the mechanics of figuring out what the problem was. Even before having his coffee, it became obvious the order of my husband's day would be to find the problem, pray it wasn't beyond hope, then fix it.

Ironically, it also would herald the beginning of one of those peculiar husband and wife conversations that makes sense only to the two people involved.

To begin with, you must understand my husband thinks out loud while tackling projects such as this one. I'm not complaining, I'm grateful he maintains everything around our home, but it's taken me more years than I'll admit to learn I don't have to answer rhetorical questions.

I was baking his favorite cookies as he sat in the kitchen, probing his way through the various possibilities. He wondered, aloud, what the three softener cycles were. Being the helpful person I am, I suggested they might be wash, rinse, and spin dry. The man has great patience!

Thereafter, the conversation, if you will, was divided half and half: his half was verbalized, mine was silently wandering. I nodded or vocally agreed from time to time, but I was off on my own interpretation of cycles, and they had little or nothing to do with repairing the softener.

"How does the electromagnet close the valves?"

Right! I'm going to answer that? He was on his way towards a resolution to the problem, and I was still stuck on cycles. There are motorcycles as well as three, five, and ten speed bicycles, not to mention unicycles and tricycles. Don't forget stationary cycles that don't go anywhere, and while we're at it, remember to recycle.

"That valve is stuck and didn't release; the natural progression was interrupted. I'll have to check the compression on the spring."

Nodding at what I hoped was an appropriate place, I continued mulling over cycles. Life is made up of cycles. The progression of events during those cycles varies from one person to the next, but otherwise, we seem to follow the same general format from start to . . .

"Only one valve is not functioning, it seems. Hmm, so that should work, shouldn't it?"

A lot of things should work, but do they always? I began to think about New Year's resolutions. There is a type of cycle there in that often we make them, we break them, then we forget them. It isn't an intentional pattern, but it often is easier than anything else we might do with them.

I couldn't help but wonder if it was going to be easier to fix the water softener than it would be to keep at least one resolution for the coming year. I also began to wonder what one thing I could resolve to carry out completely.

"*Aha!* I've found what's causing the problem!"

Now there was music to my ears! That statement got a smile as well as an enthusiastically verbalized "*all right!*" Perhaps my resolution was right there in front of me all the time and I simply hadn't recognized it.

If I became a better listener and paid closer attention to details, I'd understand more about all those things like electromagnets, brine levels, pressure levels, priming, valve releases, cycles as they pertain to water softeners.

Nah, on second thought, I might have to somehow become involved in the actual process of repairing something if I did that. I think I'll stick with baking cookies and nodding. My husband has never expected answers before when he has mused and pondered repair situations. I can't believe he is ready now to engage in any conversations with me about softener cycles or anything else mechanical.

Homemade cookies are for him a type of elixir for stress management. Rather than learning the difference between a washer and a gasket, I think perhaps I'll resolve to bake cookies at least once a week in the coming year.

I don't anticipate some type of home repair to be necessary that often, but I do believe in insurance, and cookies are a sure policy. Being prepared in any event can't be foolish.

I believe my husband and I both know exactly what the other is saying most of the time, even when it isn't said aloud. Maybe we even can say we have come "full cycle" in our relationship.

Maybe we also can say doing so was an unrecognized, unverbalized New Year's resolution we made many years ago that we didn't have much difficulty keeping at all.

Now... Who says men and women speak different languages?!

PART II

Coping With the
Technocrats

...

A CODED REMINDER OF NOMENCLATURE YOU'VE MISPLACED—November 29, 1995

To be an active, informed, functional member of the nineties, it is important to be able to encode and decode anything, preferably without a code book. I tried (unsuccessfully), to convince my mind to "listen up" to this message one day as I attempted what is considered a routine procedure practiced regularly and easily by most people.

Instead of going into the bank to cash a check, my husband and I decided to use the MAC ATM card machine. It's efficient, quick, but you have to know your own secret code.

I couldn't remember mine, my husband couldn't remember his, and neither of us could remember where we'd put the "Captain Midnight Code Book" that's supposed to remind us of our numbers when we can't remember them any other way. Unfortunately, having a numerical series *plus* a corresponding word is totally useless when you haven't a clue as to what either one is.

We could have gone into the bank with eighteen forms of identification and asked them to please look up the number, but that would have been an embarrassing option, certainly not number one on my priority list. Hence, the next option was to search all the likely places we might keep this information. You know the kind of place—logical, secure, sensible—the places I forget about first!

It's disquieting having such small things as short, four-digit sequences escape me so easily, but my friend Julie gave me an article written by Susan Reimer, from the *Baltimore Sun*, that lightened my heart considerably because it made me realize my lapses of memory are not unique.

As I read Reimer's tricks for remembering things, from making a list for *everything* (which I already do, over and over again, one in every room plus an extra in my purse at all times), to carrying around empty toothpaste tubes as a reminder to buy more, I discovered that lapses of memory and finding ways to cope with them are not unique to "age challenged people." A lot of "youngsters" who are barely past thirty don't leave home without lists.

A list scribbled on a piece of paper—a used envelope, an unused corner of a tissue, the back of a photograph, an old grocery receipt—is probably regarded as the "Stone Age" version of the computer, but it can be a reliable means of storing important information I might need some time in the near future. Keeping track of these lists does present problems, obviously, but that wasn't the immediate issue we were facing.

At the moment, we were trying to recall our MAC numbers. Obviously, they aren't exactly what one includes on a grocery list, especially since lists are such disposable (intentionally and accidentally) items. No, first, we had to find the numbers, then come up with a dependable way to remember them. Enter the acronym.

An acronym seemed like the logical way to remember our codes, but acronyms have become so common it's easy to forget they aren't *real* words. Who am I kidding, it's easy to forget a lot of things.

NATO, SEATO, NASA, RADAR, and GUI (pronounced gooey, which my husband told me I'm using to write this story), also pose another problem—I forget what the letters represent!

Take RADAR, for instance, which is RAdio Detection And Ranging, and, yes, I looked it up. I could only recall it somehow involved a radio, which makes no sense to my unscientific mind. If it did, I would be able to pick up WRMR on my microwave.

Or GUI—Graphical User Interface—I'm the user and I'm not sure exactly how, but I'm interfacing with something inhuman. I don't even want to know!

Back to the elusive MAC card numbers. We'd each been given a card with different numbers. How thoughtful. We couldn't remember one set of symbols between us, yet there we were, trying to contrive a memory gimmick using two series of numbers or words. *Duh* came to mind first!

Eventually, my husband found the hidden papers with our codes, then cleverly incorporated both words in a short phrase. One would hope between us, we'll be able to remember the phrase so now we, too, can do automated banking business like the rest of the world.

Naturally, I can't tell you our secret phrase. The truth is, I hope I can remember it next time I need it. I do know it has something to do with a famous person who did something at the wrong time. Of course, once I remember all those details, I'll have to figure out which word goes with which card—assuming I remember which two words in the phrase apply to the cards.

Sometimes, all these procedures intended to simplify and streamline daily activities do everything but! It was infinitely easier, and a lot more fun, when we had just the Captain Midnight ring and code book at our fingertips, literally.

No doubt MAC is an acronym itself, standing for something very businesslike and logical, but all I can

think of when I see or hear it is Meat And Cheese—
with pickles and a special sauce on a sesame seed bun.

THE COMMITTEE IS CALLED TO ORDER
—MAY 26, 1998

My mind has been processing things its own way for a
long time. At the impressionable age of five or six, I saw
an animated, over-simplified depiction of the inner workings of the human body. It was intended to make the
functions of the major body organs understandable.

Instead of actual organs, which cause little children
to say *Eeeeeuuuck!* there were internal service stations
with tiny humans performing appropriate tasks at each
one. The film even demonstrated how the departments
worked in conjunction with, and depended on, each other.

The concepts as presented were directed at a very
juvenile audience. Unfortunately, they remained con-
vincingly vivid in my imaginative mind far longer than
they should have. I felt quite knowledgeable being able
to visualize efficient workers with hammers tapping at
their designated posts in my ears, or others with hoses
flushing out the flotsam and jetsam in my body. By comparison, the real nuts-and-bolts of biology was much less
picturesque.

One evening, we were watching a PBS program
reserved for the fund raising drives that keep it in
existence. In the middle of Dr. Christiane Northrup's
informative presentation about living well/staying well,
she referred analogously to the committee in her head
that weighs and ponders all incoming data. I knew
instantly I'd found a common bond with this delightful
woman. *She'd* understand little people with tools
operating at their appointed stations inside the body!

I have the same kind of committees, with many diverse members, meeting in my head, too. They aren't the same ones dressed in work overalls and caps, carrying tool kits or operating conveyor belts that move blood and other stuff.

They are the goateed members of the management team who oversee production at all levels. Their spectacles slip off their noses, they carry briefcases, scratch their chins, and often are at odds with each other on what appropriate actions they should recommend to me about weighty issues. Solutions to the problems they address are seldom found in a tool kit.

I hadn't thought about my own committee members in a long time, but suddenly, there they were, quite real again, collectively cheering because a very intelligent, well-educated medical person also recognized them. We were sharing a moment of consensus about an issue of importance.

Immediately after experiencing this revelation, I began to listen more closely. My committee was teleconferencing with a person who could express Ph.D. concepts using second grade images without sacrificing the meaning or importance of the message. This was someone who understood how I collated ideas and ultimately processed information.

Shortly thereafter, my committee members convened and deliberated at great length when they realized I was toying with the notion of going public about them. Some even thought I'd be ostracized or considered a candidate for commitment—there are some issues about which they will never think as one.

But, the one thing they do agree upon is that many decisions require weighing of pros and cons, and without their collective input, I wouldn't be able to make them.

After listening to Dr. Northrup, though, I just knew there would be enough others around who host committees of their own, others who would understand, perhaps even appreciate knowing they are part of a much larger network of similar thinkers than they realize.

I'm comfortable with the simplified concept of my committee members arriving at workable solutions to issues after they've sufficiently bantered around the variables. In a way, it's as though I never have to make a decision alone.

I also believe the minds that create science fiction movies like *2001: A Space Odyssey* and *Tron* probably saw that same animation I did when I was five years old.

Do You Speak O*/ $/>&#?—June 10, 1992

The majority of us spend at least twelve years in school learning to identify and apply the twenty-six symbols of our alphabet in the process of properly learning our language. The system does have some flaws, but it has worked well as we know it for more than just a few years.

There is a certain structure on which to build, one that allows us to communicate both verbally and in writing, even when individual minds take liberties with the system.

But just as the coming of "a chicken in every pot" and "a car in every garage" created changes in our life styles, the age of "a computer in every household" has added yet another dimension to our communication system. So many of the rules of grammar as we originally learned them no longer apply now that we talk to machines, or our machines talk to other machines. *Computerese* has become a second language.

It is impossible to escape being involved with

computers, no matter how hard we try, so we may as well give in and learn something about them, if only to be able to understand our bills from utility or credit card companies.

At the supermarket our food is waved over a window called a scanner so we have the benefit of a register tape on which a computer has completely recorded our purchases.

Rarely, do we get a live person on a first call to any type of business or institution. A computer politely asks us to state our business so it can determine the nature of our needs, after which we are instructed to push the appropriate button. If we're lucky, we eventually get to talk to someone real, but that person in turn must ask his or her computer for the information we are seeking anyway.

Have you looked at your zip code directory recently? The abbreviations now listed for the names of the states are what the computer will accept, not necessarily the ones we learned in school. A computer is very particular about the number of characters it will accept for anything. For instance, there's MA, MD, ME, MI, MN, MO, and MT using no periods, please notice. Can you match up the computer abbreviations with the correct state in all instances?

If you have a long name, you already have noticed some of it is occasionally missing on those computer-generated labels seen on some of your incoming mail. This concerned me until I remembered there is an accompanying number that will separate me from the others who share the last name *Hust*.

Anyone who understands and incorporates a computer into his or her daily routine is usually quick to tell us how valuable they are, how much they can do.

This is true, so long as you know which buttons to push to make the magic work, and this is done only on the computer's terms. Getting into, moving around within, then getting back out of it, require you to know the rules of the computer.

It is absolute in its adherence to these rules and expects the same of you as a "friendly" user. If, on the other hand, you fail to follow its rules, it will become displeased, downright unfriendly, and will punish you by eliminating everything you may have attempted to accomplish with the touch of the wrong button.

Bits and *bytes* no longer refer to mosquitoes, and *default* has nothing to do with winning because the other team did not show up.

Lotus is rarely the flower or the Yoga position in conversations, and memory is the machine's, not yours.

Interfacing does not mean sewing the lining into a garment, and the *logical sector* is not the place at which you might think you are supposed to be.

Forget about trains being on these *tracks*. In fact, one of the few things I have understood thus far is that you do have to take out the garbage. It may be done differently than from kitchen to rubbish can, but the principle is basically the same.

There was a time when a garbled series of symbols were frequently found in a comic strip, when one of the characters was expressing unprintable expletives. The imagination was free to insert anything it thought suitable for the given circumstances facing the cartoon character. Now there is a very good possibility those symbols actually translate into some specific computer command.

As yet the computer and I are not on a first name basis. We don't know each other well enough for that.

Furthermore, there is no way I will communicate with it unless there is an interpreter present.

You Are Here—Maybe!—February 9, 1999

Talk about sending mixed messages! In major malls I'm supposed to think *I am Here*, but in spite of what that little star next to those words denotes, I am *nowhere*, or more accurately, and honestly, *I am Lost!*

My ability to get lost in a small room with more than one door is a given, so my infrequent excursions into the foreign world of mammoth malls make me feel more like an explorer than a shopper. In a relatively short time I begin calculating how long it will be before my family realizes I've disappeared.

Designers of these menacing structures are supposedly being considerate by strategically posting signs decorated with colorful adjacent rectangles arranged in peculiar patterns. They presume people with some sense of direction (and adventure), are the frequenters of their architectural tributes to shop-a-holics. However, once they've finished the task of constructing a mall, they never return to see whether or not the plan is working. If they did, they would have to confront angry, frustrated individuals such as I who might throttle them, after they've directed us back to the outside world.

At one time I would have congratulated myself on being able to find the store nearest the sign to use as a landmark. It often required a lot of walking and looking, and, I must confess, there were relatively few stores in the earlier complexes, but I eventually figured out where I was.

Upon entering today's malls, I try to determine, if not exactly, then sort of, where I am by the color coding, which is dumb. The stores are not painted bright red, blue, yellow, or green. I usually dismiss this approach quickly.

Even if I'm lucky enough to identify the closest store, there's no guarantee I'll find myself on the map. In some of the newer, multiple-level shopping cities, one company has several widely scattered locations within the mall. Not only am I in the wrong wing, but also on the wrong floor. For all I know I may have crossed a state line in my wandering. The designers of these mazes have sick minds.

It's rather unnerving having a sign imperiously indicating YOU ARE HERE. How can an inanimate object be so confident of *my* whereabouts? Only the star is *here,* and it chooses a different *here* on every board. If it can't figure out where *it* is, how am I supposed to figure out where *I am?*

I don't know where *I am*—but, I do know I don't want to be *here,* (wherever *here* is), and I don't know how to escape!

As if that's not insult enough, I can never find a YOU ARE HERE star near an exit. Unfortunately, when I actually find a door that will let me out, it's not the same one I entered, a challenge I face in the smallest shopping centers with only one parking lot. There's no end to my dilemma when I have to locate which store, which floor, and which door.

Regardless of how they try, they will never convince me I am *here.* I wonder if I would know how to navigate more successfully in those places if the signs read, YOU ARE NOT HERE, or FACE IT, YOU ARE LOST!

Those boards should be rigged with electronic buttons reading, PUSH IF YOU'D RATHER *NOT* BE HERE. It might be embarrassing the first few times, but if the alert summoned mall security, it would be a guaranteed way of getting out.

Of course, once I finally manage to escape to the outside world, one way or another, I then must decide which of the many lots stretching for miles in every direction is holding my car captive. In small lots I focus on external landmarks to remember where my car is parked. At mega-malls, there are no landmarks, just more cars.

Just when I think I'm about to locate my car the same day I arrived, I discover that everyone who owns the same make, model, and color as mine is also at the mall. . . .

You know, that's a whole other dilemma.

Mix 'n Match—Strange Bedfellows
—May 1,1996

Along those same lines, people interested in securing accurate, reliable information on a variety of topics know that unlimited sources are readily available to them if they just know where to look. In today's health-conscious society, for instance, hospitals are among the leaders providing affordable seminars to those who seriously want to learn and practice good health habits.

With that goal of learning in mind, my friend and I enrolled in a seminar designed to help middle-aged women minimize the discomforts of menopause. Finally, a situation where embarrassing questions could be asked; weird experiences could be shared; mutual understanding and consolation would be genuine.

Promptly on the hour, a young nurse whom I guessed was about thirty years old and within thirty minutes of delivering her first baby (give or take a time zone), walked into the lecture hall and announced she was our instructor. Quick, tell me, what's wrong with this picture?

Was she serious? Were we in the right hall? We looked at each other, back at her, and our faces clearly reflected the same reaction: "Been there, done that!" We obviously weren't on the same page, not even in the same book.

Excluding the nurse, not one of the approximately fifty women in the room was pregnant, and without an act of God, was going to be again! Ever! Period! Amen!

This class wasn't only to be about medical credentials. It was supposed to be about meeting on common ground with fellow sufferers and establishing a mutually comfortable communication zone in which to exchange helpful information. This was supposed to be about getting the straight scoop from the "horse's mouth"!

The young nurse began talking knowledgeably and enthusiastically, perhaps to instill confidence in us, or to make sure she got through her notes before the baby arrived. Either way, it didn't work.

About twenty minutes into her presentation she felt a need to leave, apologized to the group, and excused herself. End of class, arrangements for re-enrollment and/or return of money to be made through the hospital business office.

The emergency was legitimate, but her departure was so fast we simply sat and looked blankly at each other for a few seconds. Gradually, we realized regardless of the cause, we'd been deserted—left to weigh our alternatives.

Hadn't there been even *one* menopausal nurse available to coach us? The young nurse was very well informed, and in her brief presentation, offered a lot of helpful text book material to anyone who had not done much personal research.

However, most of us were hoping for someone with whom we could commiserate first hand. Clearly, she couldn't give us any inside poop. In truth, we could have coached her about what to expect as she prepared to deliver *her* baby.

Naturally, the folly of the evening's experience got me thinking about the amusement of some other teacher/student mismatches. I began to wonder how I would react if I found myself enrolled in any one of the following courses being taught by the not necessarily appropriate instructors:

"Improving Your Skills in Tact & Diplomacy, My Way or Forget It." Murphy (Geez, Guys) Brown instructing.

"Singing Lessons Guaranteed to Draw Rave Reviews" taught by the one and only (thank God), Roseanne.

"Sweeping, Avant-garde Hair Styles" taught by trend setter Don King (anyone with less than eight inches of hair see Sinead O'Connor's listing).

"Skillful Application of Make-up" with none other than Tammy Faye Bakker, (recently graduated from Clown College), instructor.

"Helpful Housecleaning Hints" by the ever popular Phyllis (leave-the-vacuum-cleaner-in-the-living-room-so-you-can-always-say-you-were-just-getting-ready-to-use-it), Diller. Serious cleaners need not waste time enrolling.

"Ten Rules for a Successful Marriage" taught by Zsa Zsa Gabor. (Dahlings, bear in mind each rule is to be applied to a different husband.)

In fairness to the young nurse, mixing old and young would surely have offered some benefits to all of us. But, in this case, I preferred to get the word straight from the mouth of an "old horse" that's already "been there, done that." Call me old fashioned, but it's awkward having someone half my age technically explaining to me how a book says I should be feeling.

Besides, I'd already read the book. I was hoping to see the stage production.

IS THERE A LAB RAT ASSIGNED TO ME?
——OCTOBER 15, 1996

How the obvious can be so easily overlooked is always a mystery to me. Recently scientists discussed the results of using Leptin, a substance they hoped would be effective in controlling weight. In simplified terms, Leptin says to the brain, "Don't eat!" The scientists said it worked on rats, but it wasn't working on humans. And this is a surprise?

Of course it doesn't work on humans. The human brain is capable of bypassing advice it chooses to ignore. If a human sees food it wants, it *de*activates its brain.

Think about it, does a rat care what it eats? Perhaps, but I'd be willing to bet that a hot fudge sundae, triple cheese pizza, and garbage are all equal in its eyes.

If it's still full from the last experimental meal, a rat probably won't eat, with or without Leptin. Yes, I do think it's possible for even a rat to get too much of a good thing. After all, how much of each test meal can the little fur ball work off in such cramped quarters?

Still, we turn to the results of tests performed on a rodent to tell us how to control our diets. Now, before I get into trouble with anyone, I honestly do know there are good rats and bad rats, and the good ones perform invaluable services. But humans and rats are different (for which I am grateful) and I have difficulty relying so greatly on a rat for a stamp of approval on the food I eat.

The average person generally knows which foods to

eat to maintain good health. Nevertheless, there are those among us who believe it's necessary to house, feed, and study little rodents in order to substantiate this information.

After a designated number of meals, these people compare rats and humans. Their findings are meant to offer us healthful, dietary guidance. If it's okay for the lab rat to eat, then it's okay for me to eat? I don't think so.

I'd like to see some greater selectivity in the choice of the testee. I'd prefer to have the results come from someone who sits at a table and eats with recognizable utensils, people I know, who speak my language. An animal in a testing lab that doesn't fully appreciate the difference between garbage and pizza is going to have trouble influencing my eating habits.

Just because a cute little rodent vacillates between beef hamburger and turkey hamburger should not be reason enough for me to alter my diet. Maybe the rat has a grudge against a cow that once stepped on its tail, or a turkey that once tried to peck at it when it got too close.

Maybe the rat retains fluids, so the cardboard-like taste of unsalted chips, nuts, and pretzels appeals to it. It probably eats cardboard all the time anyway, or at least gnaws through it. Does a rat know the difference between a tortilla chip and the box it comes in? And if it does, does it care? Either way, I have no intention of including "julienne strips of box" in my salad.

I still want to believe I have a few advantages over a rodent. Both lab rats and humans get teased, tempted, and tested everyday, but the rats don't get choices, only the humans do. I may at times lack the will power to select what's best for me, but at least I get to exercise my options when it involves the food I eat. And I'm not sure I totally agree with the findings of someone who reads a rat's vital signs.

Except for the lab people who work with them in testing situations, I don't know too many people who have good things to say about rats. Unfortunately, the majority of rats I read about eat garbage, spread disease, and generally upset everyone and everything wherever they go, and I have some difficulty separating them from their good relatives.

Yet we continue to be likened to them. I wonder if someplace there is a rat that somehow identifies with each specific human, just so its reactions personally make that individual's life miserable?

I'm convinced there must be a rat in a lab somewhere assigned to me, one that knows I love ice cream, pizza, and a lot of other foods on the questionable list. I hope it hasn't yet heard what some of its co-rats have said, "We can now safely eat peanuts!" If it has, it will feel obliged to offer a counter opinion the analysts won't be able to ignore.

The good peanut announcement will then have to be withdrawn until further tests can be performed, all because *my rat* is getting even for some of the ugly insults I've hurled its way. A rat makes a decision and I have to make a change. Just exactly who's being tested here?

A lab rat has the possibility of living a long time. It enjoys all the necessary creature comforts provided by those who want to observe it over a lengthy period, those who want to keep it safe, healthy, and alive. It's a cushy job, complete with full medical benefits, all the food it wants, and warm, clean shelter out of harm's way.

I, on the other hand, give up a food I enjoy so this pampered rodent can maintain a comfortable life style.

A lab rat may not be one of my hundred favorite animals on earth, but it's no dummy. It recognizes the hand that feeds it, and if it reacts properly, it gets to reap the benefits of a long and prosperous life.

I'd like to locate my rat to see if I can work a deal with it. All the garbage it wants in exchange for keeping ice cream, peanuts, and pizza on the good list.

If that fails, I'll personally provide the little rotter with whatever it wants for its last meal.

Incorporating New Concepts—October 5, 1999

A young man with a phone stuck to the side of his head walked in front of my parked car at a large shopping plaza. At first I thought he was making a "quickie" call on his way into one of the stores but soon discovered he was merely walking up and down the aisle chatting animatedly with someone. Scenes like this are replayed over and over, any place, any time, day after day, once again demonstrating how quickly we redesign our lives to incorporate a new concept.

The mobile or cell phone is a wonderful addition to our lives. It wasn't necessarily designed to be used only for emergencies, but I believe some individuals are in the state of advanced ridiculousness regarding the way we use these communication devices.

It's impossible to drive anywhere without seeing at least one in every ten motorists engaged in a phone conversation. I'm sure a great deal of business is being conducted, but I'm equally as sure a lot of pizzas are also being ordered.

I can't even recall the last time I made it through an entire meal in a restaurant without hearing someone's phone ring. Personally, I would draw the line on this interruption if I owned the restaurant. I really don't enjoy being part of other people's conversations in such close quarters.

The scenes that strike me as the most unusual involve individuals walking down a street (or around in a parking lot), through a mall, or riding in a crowded elevator chatting casually about nothing in particular. Is there honestly that great a need to just "reach out and touch someone?"

Examples of this nature bring out uncontrollable temptations in some of us. My husband couldn't resist an opportunity to "join 'em since we can't fight 'em, sorta."

The area over the dashboard in his van is very deep and flat, a perfect spot for him to conspicuously mount an antique black Bakelite phone, circa 1940. For the longest time, whenever he pulled up to an intersection and spotted another driver on the phone, he "answered" his phone and carried on an imaginary conversation, complete with hand gestures. A couple of times he even called out, painstakingly cranking the numbers on the slow rotary dial.

The mock gesture was worth the effort just to see the reactions of nearby drivers, who initially registered curiosity and/or wonder, especially if they were too young to immediately recognize the old style phone. After figuring out the obviously ridiculous mockery, and perhaps even agreeing the exaggerated need to communicate is sometimes carried to dumb extremes, they usually laughed.

Dealing with any new innovation evokes interesting reactions between generations. As younger people we often think we have the exclusive rights to being on the cutting edge, when, in fact, the only difference is the perspective from the opposite sides of the time line. Younger people have yet to learn that older people have already experienced the cutting edge with the new inventions they saw created.

As people age, they have another advantage: they've learned the cutting edge keeps moving. Even though many are tempted to regard most new innovations as being about as advanced as they can get, or as the song implies, "They've gone about as far as they can go," the older generation knows new and improved versions probably will appear to refine and replace them. Nevertheless, their awe continues.

Younger people, on the other hand, always seem to know each new innovation is just the beginning of greater things to come, perhaps because younger people are constantly trying to re-invent the wheel. They rarely view anything with a limited attitude, which is fortunate; that "sky's-the-limit" thinking is what keeps the wheels moving forward.

It's hard to know exactly when the younger generation becomes older, but a clue that they're relinquishing cutting-edge rights to the next generation might be when they begin wondering "what could they possibly do next?"

Will their compact phones someday be placed on the dashboards of their cars to playfully tease the younger generation communicating with—*what*?

BEWARE OF FROZEN FOG—DECEMBER 12, 1995

Whether the effect is real or imagined, a healthy slug of caffeine to jump-start the body in the morning is vitally necessary to some people. It gives the body a physical boost, and activates the mind and gets it on track. Without the benefit of this questionable elixir, some of us would go through the day, maybe even through life, never quite sure what to make of some of the things we see and hear.

Our daughter experienced a perfect example of just such bewilderment one morning as she drove to work, half listening to the radio, but more intent on arriving safely at her destination. She was looking forward to having her regular dose of caffeine since the weather had spurred her into leaving home before she'd had it there. It was the first morning winter was serious about making its presence known, so drivers were moving with exaggerated caution.

As she proceeded, she became aware of what the announcer on the radio was telling people about travel conditions: "The fog has frozen to the road, causing several accidents in the area." The fog froze? To the road?

At first she questioned what she'd heard. After all, her mind had to be a little fuzzy without its morning caffeine. The announcer continued, however, and she began to listen more carefully. Yes, he was telling people the fog had frozen to the road. That description was a first in weather forecasting as far as she knew.

I'm not a meteorologist. Perhaps fog can freeze to the road and cause accidents. Anything is possible, but you have to admit it sounds a bit strange. After she told me about her drive-time entertainment, I couldn't help but wonder if maybe the announcer just felt a need to add a bit of an unusual twist to make people sit up and take notice. If that was so, it had certainly worked in her case.

A weather forecaster is in a targeted position. There are a lot of people out in radio and television land who wait for and plan their very existence around his/her specific weather words each day. Normally intelligent, rational people hold him personally responsible for each day's meteorological happenings.

We hold a human being, a mere mortal, to his word when he attempts to make reasonably accurate predictions about Mother Nature's antics. Have we learned nothing from storms being named for females?

Many people frequently change their plans between eight in the morning and five in the evening, but those same people expect the weather person to tell them precisely what kind of weather to expect over a five day period. I find that very amusing, especially since I'm one of those people who always listens to the weather reports.

As a result of giving greater attention to weather reports than I devote to almost any other portion of the newscasts, I've spent a considerable amount of time trying to figure out exactly what forecasters mean when they attempt to differentiate, for instance, between snow showers, snow squalls, and snow flurries.

From time to time an announcer will relax and just say it's going to snow. Now, that gets my attention every time. There's some mystery surrounding the word snow all by itself and I'm left to figure out, if I'm so inclined, how much or how little, when, and in what form.

Then there's the game of determining whether we're going to get hail, sleet, freezing rain, light snow, heavy snow, wet snow, rain mixed with snow, or a sampling of all of the above. In winter especially, once a person is committed to being out and about in any kind of potentially inclement weather, it should be adequate to simply say some "nasty stuff" will be falling from the sky so we should exercise caution. I hardly think people concentrate on classifying what's falling on their windshields as they're negotiating their cars in traffic.

In the case of snow, perhaps the only thing we really need to know is whether it will amount to a couple of inches or a couple of feet. I know that would certainly help me to decide if I have to leave the house a little earlier to get somewhere, or if I'm going to be able to stay at home indefinitely and should start a 2,000 piece jigsaw puzzle!

In some respects forecasting the weather has taken on a "show biz" format featuring colorful maps diagramming the relationships between squiggly lines, moving blobs, and large H's and L's. These graphics are accompanied by enough different scientific words (What is anomalous or unanimous propagation anyway?) to offer variety for each week day.

It's probably necessary to try to spice up the reports in order to get a bigger viewing audience which in turn leads to higher ratings and more invitations to speak publicly. I guess it's a '90s kind of thing, like so many other areas, where new and improved innovations are the order of the day. I suppose I'll survive as long as I am able to translate all the current terminology into some basic words, like hot, cold, rain, snow.

A fog is silently settling in. My mind is alert because I've had more than enough caffeine today, so there can be only one explanation for that green van that just rapidly slid through the stop sign:

That doggoned fog is freezing to the road again!

Tattoo Charlie Sees The Big Picture
—November 12, 1996

If you agree frozen fog is peculiar, wait until I tell you about a rather unusual billboard along a stretch of highway in Kentucky that grabbed my full attention as soon as I saw it: TATTOO CHARLIE'S, DONE WHILE YOU WAIT!

Whoa! Excuse me, am I missing something? While you wait? Is there any other way to get a tattoo? I mean, how else can a tattoo artist draw pictures on a person's body if the person isn't waiting . . . right there . . . with his body?

Could it be no one actually thought about the ramifications of a statement like that? Did no one realize how absurd (and physically impossible) it is to have a tattoo applied if you don't wait there with your body?

Perhaps, from a marketing point of view, it was intended as an attention-getter. It certainly got mine! I didn't run to Tattoo Charlie's establishment, but my piqued mind ran off in more curious directions than I should admit.

For several miles, I tried to imagine ways, rational and otherwise, a person could get tattooed without waiting with his body while the artwork was being applied. Believe me, I couldn't think of much that would be considered even remotely reasonable. As you'll see, I got carried away.

In a rather bizarre scenario, a tattoo artist might initiate a no-wait arrangement by first faxing a sampling of pictures to a potential client. It's far-fetched but not impossible that a method already is being developed whereby he also can use the fax machine to apply the desired design.

He'd have the client fax back the selection with all

the necessary dimensions, then transpose the selected design according to the specifications and fax it back. The client would then apply it himself with the help of enclosed directions.

It would be like those paper transfers kids use to put temporary pictures on their bodies—sort of—only this would be permanent (at least, I think it would be permanent).

In time, the whole procedure might become sophisticated enough so those who weren't interested in the "do-it-yourself" method would be able to hold the fax machine up against the desired body part. He and Charlie could co-ordinate the incoming time and, *Voila!* Quick, easy, and probably painless.

As you can see, my thoughts went so far beyond ridiculous I couldn't believe I even was entertaining them, but initially, that sign really struck me as going so far beyond dumb it couldn't be ignored!

I suppose if a person had an artificial limb, they could drop it off and come back for it at a later time, depending on how long they could be comfortable without it. People decorate other body parts, too, but some are hard to separate and drop off. My mind was going way beyond any real considerations. Indeed, tattooing while you wait?

At first I thought the entire concept of truth in advertising was being challenged to the maximum. Many advertisers find ways to do that, but usually their unlikely claims aren't nearly as obvious as Tattoo Charlie's.

If we allowed ourselves to believe everything touted by some of the merchants of mendacity, we'd all be healthy, rich, beautiful, successful, overwhelmingly popular, and constantly happy.

Not only would our teeth be sparkling white and bright, they would be perfectly formed. We'd have glowing highlights in gorgeous, silken hair. Our bodies would be perfect tens. We always would smell good, feel well, dress impeccably, and be intelligent, witty, and highly personable under any and all conditions.

Some advertisers would have us believe merely buying and using their merchandise would be as close as possible to everyone's having a personal, on-command genie (complete with decorated bottle) granting unlimited wishes.

The more I mulled over Tattoo Charlie's ad, however, the more I realized that in its simplicity it was, in fact, truth in advertising. You waited or you didn't get tattooed. *Period.* Clearly, there is no other realistic way. It was just rather odd seeing a reminder that people were expected to wait with their bodies during the process. Tattoo Charlie knows more about human nature than I gave him credit for.

I'm not planning to get a tattoo from Charlie or for that matter, anyone else, but his billboard certainly caused me to think.

You know, it is just possible Charlie might be interested in expanding his business if the logistics of faxing tattoos back and forth could be worked out.

Naturally, timing would be essential. It could be extremely embarrassing to tattoo the wrong name onto someone's "dupa."

I know, *give it up!* I've already turned an innocent advertisement into something weird.

Tattoo Charlie had the right idea all along.

Sadly, because my thinking about some things has become so jaded, I just didn't recognize honesty when I saw it.

Of course, it's just possible a mistake could also be faxed back and corrected. . . . Okay, I quit.

CUTTING EDGE COOKING GADGETS—MARCH 9, 1994

Manufacturers claiming the magic of new kitchen gadgets holds a similar fascination for me. Just when I think I am familiar with every new thing available, another slightly more innovative, streamlined one comes along and grabs my attention and my wallet. It makes me crazy!

I probably was one of the last people I know to get a microwave, what I once regarded as the quintessential kitchen gadget. I maintained I neither needed nor wanted one, and it would no doubt just become a very expensive coffee warmer. I was not going to learn how to cook all over again.

Naturally, after having and learning, I became so dependent on it that when a minor problem left us without it for three days we nearly starved! I have since removed the microwave from the gadget category and given it a priority status all its own.

I never considered myself a gadget person, but the truth is surfacing. Over time, I have taken some delight in having a specific small tool for each task. However, what I discovered as I was doing some long overdue drawer and cupboard cleaning was just how many of these devices I actually own, but in reality, rarely ever use anymore.

One of my first discoveries was a plastic slicer that resembles a small washboard, guaranteed to slice any fruit or vegetable a person chooses to slide across it. I was amused with it for awhile, but I am uncomfortable with anything sharp in my hands. My reputation for carelessness with blunt butter knives makes my family cringe.

The same was true for the handy-dandy french fry cutter, another forgotten relic from the past. I seldom ever deep-fry anything, so that one no longer poses threats to my cholesterol or my fingertips. It and the vegetable slicer were returned to the back of the drawer after the cleaning.

Next was the pasta maker, another novelty with which I dabbled briefly. By the time I finally (barely) learned how to get the dough just the right consistency, I found I could just as easily buy good, ready-made noodles.

Furthermore, I could stop worrying about anything foreign lurking on the parts of the machine that would taint my pasta. In an effort to keep it clean, I forced more loaves of bread than noodle dough through that thing! I made a note to send that item to my daughter!

Further searching in the nooks and crannies of the drawers turned up unused cherry pitters and strawberry stem pluckers, as well as long-forgotten lettuce and apple corers. Delving deeper turned up a tomato slicer, an egg slicer, an egg chopper, and an egg separator. Besides orange, apple, and grapefruit peelers, I also found a potato peeler, a potato ricer, and a potato masher, although I rarely peel, rice, or mash anything anymore.

A pastry crimper, a pastry blender, and a hand-held type of can opener were but a few of the other white elephants still taking up drawer space. I'm not sure why, but I was unable to dispose of them, so I merely returned them to the drawer—at least until I'm moved to clean again.

The novelty of small hand gadgets seems to wear off rapidly for me. It's wonderful to have them available, but it has become abundantly clear that when I am preparing meals I tend to use two items more than any others: a stainless steel fork and a wooden spoon. Short of flipping pancakes (for which I keep the number three most important tool, a turner), there is almost nothing that can't be achieved with these reliable standbys.

To me, they are indispensable items. And I can't cut myself with them, either. (Tool number four is a dreadfully dull paring knife, the only kind I'll use).

Not long after the drawer-cleaning experience, I attended a home demonstration party at which a lovely woman named Sara Lee (her real name, honest-to-goodness!) had a gadget or gizmo for anything you can think of, and maybe eighty-five things you might not know exist. As I watched her chip, chop, snip, crimp, dice, slice, and produce fancy displays of food, I was momentarily moved to purchase one of everything until I remembered "the drawer."

I already had about ninety percent of those same items stashed somewhere in my kitchen, unused, a heartbeat and an impulsive decision away from a garage sale. I was sharply reminded that my imagination is the only thing that works to create magnificent culinary creations with those clever gadgets. What I actually do when I get them home is find convenient storage places.

Since that evening I have continued preparing our daily meals with my reliable fork and spoon. Occasionally I wonder if I might turn out something closer to spectacular with a selection from the gadget drawer. However, upon further consideration, I realize I'm no longer into "spectacular."

We know what to expect of my style of cooking which is basic, simple, and reliable. "Spectacular" now comes from a chef in a restaurant!

An Alarming Situation—November 11, 1997

The mother of all gadgets made its bid for my attention on a bleak Monday morning, the day of the week most people would vote to outlaw if given an opportunity.

Normally, I launch into each new work week knowing pretty much what to expect, but once in awhile, that unexpected annoyance upsets the balance of my day. Just about the time I think my agenda is running smoothly and I've got my personal plans under control, along comes one of those chinks in the foundation of my thinking.

In this case, a bleak Monday morning was fraught with a series of typical minor aggravations, but one in particular ultimately produced, "Why me?"

I'd set out, bent on accomplishing everything in record time, which should have been a clue in itself. After searching in vain for so-called common items, I needed to move along on my list to avoid getting bogged down. I wasn't totally discouraged yet, but I was hovering dangerously close to the edge.

I attempted a few more stops, headed for the bank, eventually found a legitimate parking place, completed my business, then prepared to drive on. My car had other plans.

I got in, inserted the key in the ignition, and for a full five minutes frantically tried to master a crash course in disarming the alarm my traitorous vehicle activated.

I didn't break anything to get into the car, and I am convinced to this day, that I did what I normally do when I approach my locked automobile. I don't have a clue what happened, but as I sat in my own familiar car, it was announcing to everyone on The Square in town that it was in jeopardy of being assaulted or vandalized.

I thought my car and I were on good terms. I naively accepted the comfortable, unspoken arrangement that, as long as I treated it with care, it in turn would perform well for me. It obviously had another agenda of which I was unaware, one that would free it from the control of the individuals who caringly feed, bathe, and protect it from the elements. It was exerting its independence . . . and winning.

I couldn't believe I was engaged in a power struggle with a parked automobile, but that's basically what it came down to. My car and I were exchanging words, so to speak.

I accused it of being a spoiled, tantrum-throwing, power-hungry, control freak that was being blatantly disrespectful. With all the improvements made to it over the years, had no pride been instilled in its workings.

It ignored my comments and responded by noisily pointing out through its warning device that this was clearly one more example of how humans shoot themselves in the foot by constantly creating new, innovative technological devices capable of stripping them of power.

It's true. In our quest to improve, advance, and better the quality of our lives, we're gradually relinquishing our control to mechanical and/or electronic equipment. We install miniscule computer chips in "things" that can apparently be parlayed into powerful forces. In this instance, my car was attempting a take-over.

After what felt like an eternity of embarrassment and frustration, I found the place in the owner's manual detailing how to deactivate the security system, stopped the dreadful noise, then drove off in my four-wheeled Benedict Arnold with as much disheveled dignity as I could muster.

It wasn't until much later in the day, when I looked

back in retrospect at what had occurred, that I realized my alarm had figuratively fallen on deaf ears.

People walking past could easily see me fumbling, and hear the raucous blaring of the alarm. Perhaps they quickly sized up the situation and merely dismissed it as another person who didn't understand the inner workings of her car. I will assume that was the case, and that others inside the buildings who could hear the noise also arrived at the same conclusion. Nevertheless, it surprised me.

Did my circumstance cause any irritation because of the noise pollution, or did I momentarily provide any entertainment to other slow-starting soldiers fighting their way through the trenches of a miserable Monday morning?

If it had continued much longer, would the noxious noise have netted me a ticket for disturbing the peace?

Were the spectators to my dilemma correct to conclude without further investigation there was no cause for alarm, it was just another errant security system gone awry?

Had it been a real emergency, would anyone have recognized it as such, or would it have been ignored, using the rationale someone else will step in to help or call the police? I thought of a television commercial in which a prudent woman advises her husband, "No, no, *you* never stop!"

Cautiously I ask, is there a prevailing attitude that still warns onlookers not to get involved, and, even more curiously I wonder, would I have felt secure if someone had approached my car to offer assistance?

Thankfully, it was harmless, embarrassing, and I can laugh at my predicament. But I will probably always wonder.

TRESPASSING IN FOREIGN TERRITORY
—NOVEMBER 7,1992

This rapid escalation of highly technical improvements has made even a television set more complicated than I'm comfortable with. Fortunately, I spend relatively little time watching it, mainly because I can't sit still very long, and when I do watch, I'm often doing something else at the same time. My mother once would have described me as having "ants in my pants."

I leave the channel-surfing to my husband and simply tune into whatever happens to be on the screen. There are few programs we see in their entirety. I have learned most commercials air at about the same time on all channels.

One evening a few years ago, when my husband was out of town, I made an uncharacteristic decision to watch an old movie favorite he had taped. My familiarity with the VCR is more than limited; even my dealings with the remote control are pretty much limited to On, Off, Volume, and arrowing up or down to find a channel. Simple is a good thing.

I had observed my husband many times as he'd manipulated the various buttons on the VCR, but never paid very close attention. No problem. I just got out the manual and read the instructions.

They seemed reasonably simple so I proceeded to follow them , step by step. Nothing happened. I read the directions again, did exactly what the book said—*nothing*.

I went through this exercise in futility repeatedly for about half and hour, then did what I should have done sooner: placed a long distance call to my husband! I explained to him exactly what I was doing. He didn't understand why it wasn't working. He was quite sure the VCR was in working order. Trying desperately to solve my dilemma, he asked, "Are you *sure* you pushed zero four first?"

What "zero" four?

The manual didn't say zero four. The manual said "Channel 4," no 0, or zero, or aught—nothing! Obviously, after much stammering and fussing about the inaccuracy of the wording in the manual, I conceded that I had only been pushing the number four.

There is no sense in trying to explain why I would assume anything other than what I saw in print. When I finally entered zero four (04), I got to enjoy my movie (so, I wanted to see *White Christmas* in the middle of the summer—I happen to be a Danny Kaye fan!)

One of the many times you-know-who told this tale to friends, a very young, overly intelligent child questioned how I could not know I had to push the zero. The younger generation takes modern technology for granted, along with fast food and credit cards.

Most of them could perform programming gymnastics before entering kindergarten! At that age I still believed a mouse squeaked, ran around where it didn't belong, and was something to be caught in a trap! The big, green eye on the Zenith Radio was as technologically fascinating as it got!

That whole remote control concept has more going against it than for it as far as I'm concerned. I thought the original ones with a limited number of buttons were bad enough, mainly because it made a channel surfer out of my husband and just added to my disenchantment with television.

But the most recent models combine so many functions for both the television and the VCR that a simple, direct instruction book is out of the question. Apparently, *it* assumes the user is "remote-control" literate.

And there are so many compactly arranged buttons offering so many options on that evil stick. Even if I knew what to push, it would be nearly impossible for me to push only one instead of three or four all at the same time. It may as well be as small as those tiny per-form-every-function-you-can-name wristwatches with buttons that can only be pressed with the tip of a pointed object. Did Dick Tracy have this much trouble with his two-way wrist-radio?

All this serves to reinforce my theory these gadgets are strictly for younger people and men. They've been designed in such a way that more mature women will quickly lose interest in their use.

Men, on the other hand, may not really be any more efficient at operating them, but rapid channel surfing covers up a lot of mistakenly pushed buttons, and it gives them unlimited control of the television.

Unfortunately, it also reinforces some people's thinking that many women aren't capable of grasping some technical concepts. Obviously, I, and others like me, would prefer to believe there are some things women are not especially interested in doing.

But I'm curious. If men are more capable of learning about advanced technology, why can't they master the simple technique involved in putting down the toilet seat?

PRESSING TWO FOR INFORMATION—MARCH 18, 1997

Usually my husband has little or no problem dealing with modern technology, but one day he stormed into the kitchen with an imprint of the telephone receiver embossed on his ear and said, "You really ought to write about trying to get information over the phone!"

He was more than serious, and beyond mere frustration! In our house, he handles all the research done by phone, whether it's to find car or vacuum cleaner parts, correct a questionable bill, or compare insurance rates.

On that particular morning, he had been trying to call a *well-known* electronics company to ask a simple question.

He dialed, and a recorded message thanked him for calling the *well-known* company, then instructed him to: "Please push One if he wanted to talk with someone in sales, Two if he wanted to talk with someone in repair and service, Three if he needed installation information. He pushed Two.

A second polite computer-generated voice thanked him again, then directed him to: "Please push One if he wanted information regarding televisions, Two for telephones, Three for computers, Four for VCRs . . . he didn't wait for the entire menu, he just pushed Two.

Again he was thanked, then offered a third menu: "Please press One for standard phones, Two for cordless phones, Three for cell phones"—the voices always said "please."

He pushed Two, was thanked, then told by a fourth voice, "All our customer representatives are busy at the moment. Please stay on the line, your call will be answered in the order in which it was received." Yeah, right!

After about fifteen minutes the alternating music and commercials stopped. He was poised to push Two again, out of habit, but caught himself in time when he realized he was then getting a busy signal.

After a few choice words, he started all over again. He succeeded, finally, in reaching a live person who offered some possible reasons for the cause of the problem—no solutions, just suggestions—may be, could be, sorry.

An amusing (if frustrating), suspicion he harbors about this routine is that each company or place of business has only one customer "rep" frantically fielding all calls as they come in. My husband has made more than one call to different departments in the same company several times, and swears he recognizes the same, familiar voice offering him information, transferring or referring him to another department, or taking his orders.

The big corporations are not the only ones who use this means of handling customer needs. Medical offices, banks, department stores—they've all installed computerized telephone receptionists who divert callers into holding patterns in limbo, supposedly to be entertained with music and inviting advertisements. Where is it all going to end?

Because my husband spends a great deal of time pressing phone buttons, following instructions from people who aren't bodily on the other end of the line, and waiting, his frustration often leads his imagination down the path of worst case scenario regarding his time on the phone.

For instance, what if at the Pearly Gates there is a telephone with *The Number* to call for final information?

He dials.

"Thank you for calling God. If you are Catholic, please press One and have a list of your sins ready; Protestant, press Two and have your mother's maiden name and social security available for identification; Hindu, press Three and present your three next-life choices, in order of preference; Jewish, press Four without guilt; Atheist, we're sorry, you have the wrong number . . . "

He presses Two.

"Thank you for pressing Protestant. If you are a Baptist, please press One, an Episcopalian, press Two, a Lutheran, press Three, a Methodist, press Four . . . "

He presses Two, again.

"Thank you for being an Episcopalian. If you are Charismatic, please press One, Standard old 1928 prayer book Episcopalian, press Two . . . "

He presses Two.

"Thank you for calling God. She's on another line right now. If you wish to remain on the line and wait, please press one; if you wish to have Her return your call, press Two and leave your name, number, and the reason for your call; if you would like to be transferred to Her voice mail, press Three. . . ." Several minutes later, "Please hold, Sir, *your* call is now being transferred to the *Hot Line* . . ."

He tries frantically to press Two again, but it's too late! She already knows who he is and why he's calling.

A deep, ominous voice says, "Thank you for calling. You have been transferred to H—."

THE FACTS OF LIFE, SENIOR EDITION
—DECEMBER 9, 1997

Some situations, involving modern technology or not, are harder than others to accept. However, many people of maturity arbitrarily choose the half century mark to finally relent and acknowledge certain of these occurrences are facts of life about which we really have little or no choice.

I held out for several more years, all the while hoping perhaps the odds might eventually turn around and be in my favor. I wasn't yet prepared to accept or reckon with what other's considered unavoidable or predictable.

After sixty-plus years I have come to terms with the inevitable: I was wrong. The odds didn't change, and neither did the predictable situations.

Therefore, I share with you some of the observations I am at long last recognizing as the way it really is.

- A new house gets just as dirty as the old one you left behind.

- No matter how dry and brown the grass gets in late summer, the weeds will flourish.

- A road detour inevitably goes in the opposite direction of your destination. Venture off on your own and you either get lost or run into another detour. Either way, it's not an adventure.

- Every food you enjoy has been banned by your doctor or condemned by the FDA.

- All the funny parts of a movie are shown during the previews.

- Metamucil has become a basic food group.

- The popcorn runs out before the movie ends.

- In a restaurant, after finally deciding to order the stuffed cabbage rolls instead of the pork chops, the last portion of cabbage rolls is being served at the next table.

- The shirt you need is the one that didn't get washed.

- If you answer the phone, it's not for you.

- Even if your weight has not changed so much as an ounce, your body has taken the liberty of rearranging it.

- If you run from outdoors to answer the phone before it stops ringing, it's a wrong number or a telemarketer.

- Wire clothes hangers multiply.

- People feel compelled to leave one square of toilet tissue on the tube so they won't have to change the roll.
- Ditto for paper towels.
- You pull up to a six-way intersection with timed lights just as your lane turns red and have enough time to work *The New York Times* crossword puzzle before the very long sequence is completed and you get another green light.
- A weather advisory interrupts regular programming just as Alex Trebek is about to give the question to the final jeopardy answer you don't know and all three contestants missed.
- You and your mate meet someone at the store, carry on an animated conversation for ten minutes, then walk away not having the foggiest idea who you've been talking to. You both assumed the other knew the person.
- If you manage to get into a check-out line behind an individual with only two items, one needs a price check.
- All your clothes shrink at the same time.
- Eat one bite of poppyseed roll from the buffet table and spend the rest of the evening with a highly visible black spot on a front tooth.
- It is impossible to go into a grocery store and buy only one item.
- All diets begin tomorrow.
- People who travel the Skyline Drive in Chicago at rush hour are either robots, test dummies, or crazy.
- The prices of gasoline and ice cream cones always increase when we need them the most.
- The last check on the pad is the one you wrote yesterday, which you forgot until you got to the register on today's shopping excursion.

- The clothes you packed into the suitcase before the vacation won't fit back in for the return trip home.
- Regardless of what time it is, it's time to eat.
- The best books at the library are all checked out, and the bookstores are temporarily sold out.
- There is almost no rerun on TV worth watching.
- The person who successfully converts dust and weeds into marketable commodities will achieve sainthood.
- Your selective hearing is often mistaken for hearing loss when, in fact, you can hear every comment excusing your hearing loss as a result of old age.

If you rank among those who already accept these snippets as truths, you may as well get prepared for yet another: You may not be over the hill, but you're sure as heck standing at the top of it!

On the bright side, the top is a broad place with a terrific view in a lot of rewarding directions you can enjoy for a long time. Another time I'll tell you about the great discoveries I made when I got there.

An Electric Mousetrap—July 11, 1995

Another unavoidable event in life is having mousetrap days. You may be familiar with them. They're triggered by the malfunctioning of important things on which we seriously rely, like automobiles, electric skillets, ballpoint pens, or anything battery operated. An object of discontent causing me a serious mousetrap day(s) was an electric typewriter on which I relied heavily. When it became non-functional, I was more than a little nonplussed.

I have owned and used a typewriter for more than forty-five years. Probably the only thing I use more is my toothbrush! My parents gave me a wonderful little manual Royal portable which reliably served me both personally and professionally throughout high school, college, and for all the years I taught. I still own this little machine.

One Christmas my husband bought me an electric typewriter. I was ecstatic! The little Royal was ceremoniously retired to a closet, and I entered the automated world of light-touch typing. Life was good!

One morning about five years later, I turned on my mechanical marvel and it growled at me. I was both angry and concerned. At that point I still regarded it as a new machine. We took it back to the place where it had been purchased and were told the typewriter doctor would have to check it out when he came in, which was only certain evenings a week.

We left the machine in the typewriter hospital for two nights, then returned when we were called to come in for a consultation. Dr. Fixit hmmm-ed several times, told us he'd performed a battery of tests, and it would cost us seventy-five dollars to replace something on the circuit board. We agreed, he performed the operation, and we took the typewriter back home. Everything was once more right with the world.

One day, less than two years after that "surgery," I was confronted with the same problem. I flipped on the switch and it began to growl at me again. Terrific! Just what I needed: a typewriter with an attitude. This time I skipped the concerned part and went straight to angry. It definitely was not a Kodak moment!

My husband called the typewriter place once again. Remember, he's the phone negotiator—I would have gone from calmly sensible to hysterically angry in less than sixty seconds! Of course, he was told we'd have to bring it in for Dr. Fixit to examine and run tests on it.

After a few minutes of stalling dialogue, in deference to me, my husband told him we'd think about it. He searched for and discovered an 800 number and decided to give it a try. No surprise, after the opening exchanges, he was referred to the local dealer. But the cutting insult came when, just before hanging up, the woman had the audacity to say it was, after all, a very old typewriter.

How dare she?! Six and a half years is very far from being over the hill. My Royal is almost fifty years old and I wouldn't insult it by saying that. It has achieved senior status and still works, dependably, I might add! I know, because I had to reclaim it from the closet and press it back into service!

What we have in the electric typewriter is an unreliable piece of equipment, or to be more politically correct, an electric typewriter that is mechanically challenged. What a cop-out! This is built-in obsolescence, modern technological blackmail!

The machine had been treated very gently, had never been banged around in the trunk of a car while being dragged between locations, was always kept covered, and had regularly been fed expensive cartridges (which, incidentally, last a very short time compared to the old inky ribbons of my trustworthy Royal). In short, it had been pampered, yet it didn't have what was required to make it serviceable longer than a few years.

My husband finally took it back to the typewriter hospital only this time without me—I wasn't prepared to deal with what I knew they'd say. There would be the familiar hmmming, followed by informing us it would have to be kept at least overnight to perform tests before a definite diagnosis could be made. I already knew what that diagnosis was going to be: replace that same something in the circuit board, "Seventy-five dollars, please," (or more, to account for inflation).

Certainly, there could be no guarantees this wouldn't happen again. Yet I wasn't convinced it was worth paying the exorbitant price of maintaining something so temperamental. It's a form of extortion which may continue to fuel the economy, but I need a more trustworthy product that will last longer than six years in exchange for this concession.

I refuse to believe we lack the ability in this country to build quality products. I was just going to tell Dr. Fixit I could and would find someone else who specialized in building better mousetraps.

I know there are still Fords and Edisons out there who are capable of producing workmanship of which they can be proud, people who do not settle for merely average.

Perhaps we all need to be reminded from time to time that average is as close to the bottom as it is to the top.

AT THE END OF MY RIBBON—AUGUST 8, 1995

Chapter two of what rapidly became "the ongoing saga of the typewriter from Hell," took on new dimensions each day.

My six and a half year old electric "typewriter with an attitude," was returned to the hospital for mechanically impaired objects for the second time to no avail. It still growled at me. I had no way of knowing whether or not a third visit would be the charm, but each successive trip forced me to draw unkind conclusions about this entire process.

First, my machine had to be numbered among the criminally insane of mechanical devices with problems.

There could be no other explanation for a machine with its bizarre behavior. My husband took the errant machine in and it demonstrated its deviant antics for the women who admitted it, but when Dr. Fixit examined it, the machine gave no indications of having any loose screws, literally or figuratively.

He no doubt transferred it to a special section of the repair hospital, and even got a second opinion from another person in the field. Try as they would to catch it off guard, the machine performed beautifully! Reliably! On command! After a week of tests they were forced to admit they could find nothing wrong with it and released it, in my custody, as functionally sound.

I had my suspicions. Even before we left the repair hospital I had decided the machine was going to be on probation. We brought it back home, carefully set it up and plugged it in, and the blasted thing growled at me again! I started having devious thoughts of my own.

Second, as a result of all these shenanigans, I concluded that giving anything mechanical the power to perform automatically also gives it the power to act on its own behalf, or not act, whichever it chooses. We're told a machine is capable of performing only what is programmed into it, but I suspect that might be an out and out lie.

Someone put a circuit board into this piece of plastic to give it the capacity to function automatically. The machine acquired the ability to diabolically upset my mere human mind and keep me at its mercy. It was bent on engaging me in a power struggle. I hate to admit it, but it succeeded.

Third, if I had to get such a seemingly willful creature, why couldn't it have been more like an R2D2 or a C3PO. I didn't need a constant challenge that grew into a contest of huge proportions between person and thing. I didn't enjoy admitting I was struggling with a machine I should be able to control.

That typewriter had to be under the influence of an evil alien or it was the devil-baby of Rosemary Robot. Exorcism was just one of the drastic alternatives I contemplated if the last repair trip proved to be futile. Beheading or driving a stake through its heart were just two of the other options up for consideration.

This monster machine got out of control and I was following closely behind it! It caused me serious frustration. I attempted to cope, but it was difficult to remain patient with a seemingly free-spirited machine whose only apparent function was to cause me grief.

But then, perhaps I was being a little too hard on it.

I suppose there was the distinct possibility that after all the testing I would be told I was overly severe in being so critical. What if what I was calling a free spirit turned out to be free radicals instead? Maybe my machine had been growling because it had been in pain, and it had no other way of communicating that message to me. I had been blaming everyone and everything from the manufacturer to malevolent forces for inflicting such inconvenience on me through an inferior, shoddily made product.

If that turned out to be the case, I would owe the machine a public apology for being so insensitive. Next these unfair, harsh feelings would send me on a guilt trip of major proportions, the kind of trip I voluntarily take easily and frequently. I'd have to go to great lengths, jumping through hoops along the way, attempting to rectify the damage and suffering I inflicted with my selfish statements, expecting a machine to perform when it was, perhaps legitimately, incapable of doing so.

Good grief, listen to what happened to me?! I was reliving that miserable experience of being on the verge of assuming the blame for someone else's poor quality of workmanship, apologizing and asking for forgiveness for something I had nothing to do with. I came dangerously close to groveling!

I told you this machine had a compelling power. It engaged me in a game of wits in which it maintained the advantage until we permanently parted company.

It was my only recourse. I found myself checking the programs and services at rehabilitation centers to see if they had provisions for dysfunctional machines and the people who try to run them.

One step away from Montel. . . .

BLANK(ET) STATEMENTS—JUNE 9, 1998

It took awhile, but my "typewriter from Hell" taught me a lesson about holding my ground when I had an opinion. I also decided I could express opinions, or not, if I felt so inclined, and there are many ways in which to do so.

Today, an interesting avenue for expressing opinions and making personal statements is by splashing those sentiments on the fronts and backs of casual clothing.

These easily changeable "bumper stickers for the body" displaying clever quips and cute drawings are subject to the daily moods, conditions and circumstances, of the wearer. There is no question when I'm prompted to wear my BROUGHT TO YOU TODAY THROUGH THE MIRACLE OF CAFFEINE shirt.

Although my own wardrobe is made up mostly of blank garments, I admit there are specific comments I'd wear on certain days if I had them. Their messages would be intended to provide little more than simple amusement, although, occasionally, I, too, would be making a statement.

HAND OVER ALL THE CHOCOLATE AND NO ONE WILL GET HURT. A day without coffee is unbearable, but a day without chocolate is impossible. Chocolate deprivation is not a pretty sight.

A GOLFER AND A NORMAL PERSON LIVE HERE. You can probably figure this one out, but here's a little clue: I don't golf. Caution: one deprived of chocolate plus one having a bad golf day equals two "non-normal" people.

AN ATTITUDE IS A TERRIBLE THING TO WASTE. Repeated wearings would make it necessary to have several copies of this one. The attitude is a family trait that keeps getting handed down from generation to generation, and we tend not to be wasteful of anything whenever possible.

BAD SPELLERS OF THE WORLD UNITE. A favorite, and a reminder to always chick, click, cluck, chuck, chEck. . . .

CAUTION:WWW.OLD.COM ATTEMPTING NEW TRICKS.COM. The computer and I still speak in different tongues, but it's beginning to learn how I do things.

OVER WHAT HILL? WHERE? WHEN? I DON'T REMEMBER ANY HILL. I decided long ago to avoid the challenge of all hills and stay on flat terrain. If I admit to being over the hill, I can only be heading in one direction.

DON'T BOTHER ME I'M CRABBY. As if anyone wouldn't be able to tell?? Of course, if it's the other way around. . . .

IF YOU ARE GROUCHY, IRRITABLE, OR JUST PLAIN MEAN, THERE WILL BE A $10 CHARGE FOR PUTTING UP WITH YOU. If only it were possible to collect on this. An appropriate retaliation might be: AN OLD GRUMP AND BEAUTIFUL PERSON LIVE HERE. Let's face it, though, I'd have to share this shirt—heck, I'd probably never get it back!

I CAN ONLY PLEASE ONE PERSON PER DAY. TODAY IS NOT YOUR DAY. TOMORROW IS NOT LOOKING GOOD EITHER. Actually, some days I can't even meet my quota of one! However, when all else fails, the newest "excuse" will do nicely: EL NINO MADE ME DO IT. Who could argue with that?

As much fun as these picturesque shirts are, they will never entirely replace the blank ones in my wardrobe. The absence of any sentiment on my shirt might make me appear to be "statement challenged" to some people, but I seriously doubt it. Besides, I can't abandon the blank ones, their silence definitely serves a distinctly different function.

Believe it or not, there are some days when I just don't feel like talking to anybody very much.

PART III

Enjoying the Ride
Between Potholes

■ ■ ■

SOME FIRST MAKE LASTING IMPRESSIONS
—APRIL 16, 1992

First experiences happen to everyone. Some of them are less important than others and are soon forgotten, while the impact of others is so overwhelming the memory of them never does fade. Such was the case with a first I experienced in the fall of 1957, a major milestone in my life: my very first day in a classroom as a new teacher.

There was absolutely nothing ordinary about this particular day. I was academically prepared, but I was dealing with other circumstances that were adding greatly to my personal anxiety.

For one thing, I was in Harlingen, Texas, roughly thirty miles north of Mexico, about twenty-five hundred miles from Ohio and home. My husband was stationed at the Air Force base, and my teaching career was to become launched at one of the local schools, James Bowie. Incidentally, it is pronounced Boo, as in Halloween, not Bo, as in Jangles. That was one of the first things I learned that morning.

It was the Monday after Halloween, and I was to take over a sixth grade class from a teacher whose husband was being relocated. My accent, which I didn't even know I had, made me easily and immediately identifiable as the new Yankee teacher, a position on that staff I shared with no one else. Furthermore, I had the audacity to pronounce my name the same as the Texas city, even though I spelled it incorrectly, no doubt attributed to my being from the North.

Eventually, most people accepted my name, even improperly spelled, but a few diehards never did stop calling me Mrs. Husston, as though the word "us" was in the first syllable.

I didn't expect that first day to be easy. Most students do not react well to substitutes or replacements, and since they had lost a teacher of whom they were very fond, I anticipated some resistance from them.

I'd reviewed names and seating charts so the thirty-six pupils would not be totally unfamiliar, but I was nowhere near well enough prepared for the displeased reactions when they discovered *their* Mrs. Taylor was being replaced by a *Yankee!*

Without a doubt, I was intimidated. To begin with, most of them were physically bigger than I. A later check of birth dates indicated the age range was from eleven (of which there were very few), to fifteen, with the majority between twelve and thirteen. I soon learned many Spanish-American children started first grade with no knowledge of English, so promotions were delayed until they became fluent enough to deal with the material presented.

I was anxious to gain their confidence, and they were equally as anxious to test my mettle. No one would easily step into Mrs. Taylor's shoes, especially *not a Yankee.*

They were subtle, I'll give them that, but they gave me difficulties right from the start, making annoying comments and criticisms, constantly reminding me Mrs. Taylor did things differently than the way I was doing them. When they weren't comparing the two of us, they engaged in loud-whispered conversations amongst themselves (in Spanish), as though I didn't even exist at the front of the classroom.

Inwardly, I was becoming desperate in the face of their challenges! If they succeeded in gaining control that first day, the school year would last an eternity. I made an impulsive decision to gamble and go for broke.

I turned to an older girl who appeared to be in charge

of the well organized rebellion they were staging, looked directly into her eyes, and, with as much courage and conviction as I could muster in a quiet but very firm voice said, "Senorita Conchetta, cerre la bocca por favor!"

She stopped talking, as did everyone else, and stared at me for five seconds before saying (to no one in particular), "Oh, Dio, the Yankee teacher speaks Spanish!"

During those five seconds I had been praying very hard to the same Dio that I had correctly remembered the phrase my own high school Spanish teacher used when she wanted us to close our mouths. Following Conchetta's response, I only hoped she hadn't seen me let out a sigh of thankful relief.

With feigned confidence, I turned and instructed the slightly bewildered class to open their social studies books to a given page, but I didn't leave that spot where I stood for at least five minutes. My legs wouldn't have moved if that building had been on fire!

Gradually, they came to accept me even though I was a Yankee, and I honestly can say by the end of the year, Louis, Reynaldo, Alex, Nancy, Juan, Phillip, Julio, Maria, Jesus, and all the rest became my friends. We had a good year together, but I have always felt just a little deceitful about that first day.

After my gamble, I never spoke Spanish again. If I had, they would have discovered my conversational knowledge of the language was limited to little more than *buenos tarde, adios, manana,* and *taco!*

When In Rome, Y'All Listen Carefully
—September 7, 1999

A limited command of conversational Spanish isn't my only language handicap. A trip south reminded me how

easily language differences can cause narrow minded-
ness. We stopped to ask directions in an unfamiliar town,
and my decoding system immediately malfunctioned. I
was sure the Southern alphabet was missing essential
letters, forgetting that "Northern Ohio Speak" is not the
universal language.

My husband asked a woman how to reach a certain
area. She asked if we knew "whay the cote hahs" was.
Initially, I thought that was a stupid question. Here we
were strangers in town, asking directions, so the odds
of our knowing the location of "cote hahs" were slim.
Thankfully, I reserved my unfair opinion. She was being
sincerely helpful, and was no doubt equally as confused
by our accent, even though we talk like the people on
television.

I picture everything about the Southern approach
to life being so unhurried, leisurely, casual . . . I am so
wrong. There was absolutely nothing slow about this
fine woman's speech. I don't know how fast she types,
but she speaks at least 240 words per minute. Between
that and her accent, I was lost after the first six syllables.

Ironically, she mentioned having trouble understanding her husband because he talks so fast. In fact,
she always recaps important conversations, just to be
safe. Their conversations must sound like a tape being
fast-forwarded.

While my husband assumed the task of interpreter
(that comes under the same heading as phone negotiator,
thank goodness), I began chatting with another friendly
woman about the nearby river. She politely corrected
my mispronunciation of its five-letter name.

No matter how hard I worked at it, I couldn't make
it sound right. It was a challenge for this born and bred
Northerner to reinterpret familiar phonetic symbols into

uniquely different sounds. We laughed, but after that I waited quietly as my husband handled any further dialogue.

After an entire afternoon of working to translate the strange sounds, we ventured into a local restaurant where I planned to point at the menu and just skip further verbal communications. Silence is often my best line of defense.

We were greeted and seated—so far so good, very few actual words had been exchanged. When the waitress came to take our orders, my husband asked about a local site. She smiled and said, "I'm sorry, I don't know, I'm from Ohio." I was ecstatic! I understood every word!

Throughout the meal we had several quick exchanges with her. She said she was from Kent, but when we said we were from Medina, she admitted she was actually from Randolph, a town with which few people outside the region are familiar.

We discussed how she was adjusting to the regional differences. One example she shared took place the first day she appeared at work with a curly hair style. A coworker complimented her, prefacing the comment with, "Y'all've rowed up yo haiyeh!" The waitress thought a moment, then said, "Oh, you mean *curled* it." Her Southern friend laughed at the funny way she said things.

The following day she took in the box and emphatically pronounced the word "curling," not "rowing" iron as she pointed to it on the box. Again, the Southerner laughed at how "puh-cule-yuh Nawthuhners talk."

The point was made, but for awhile, the waitress routinely called her Ohio sister and spoke in exaggerated, clearly enunciated words, asking if she still "sounded like a Northerner." She liked her new friends and surroundings, but wasn't ready to abandon her roots.

She soon learned she didn't have to. She recognized the importance of roots, others' as well as hers, but best of all, she understood and accepted some differences can be compatibly shared, even if not in the same language.

That day we did, in fact, locate the "cote hahs" (court house) and reach our destination, thanks to the directions from the friendly, helpful woman with whom we first spoke. But of greater importance was my coming away with a renewed respect for, and more of an open mind about, differences that may not be so different, after all.

When in Rome, *ravioli*; Poland, *pierogie*; China, *won tons*. Different words, same thing . . . close enough.

DECOR BY ANY OTHER NAME—SEPTEMBER 1, 1997

At some time or another in my life I've lacked the experience to make clear-cut distinctions about several things. As a young wife I was nonplussed when asked about my choice of home decor. Many young women I knew or met in the early years of our marriage seemed to have very definite ideas of how they were going to decorate their homes or apartments. Furthermore, their ideas had specific names.

I honestly had not ever thought about what kind of furniture I would want someday. We were not in a position to purchase many new furnishings, and until we were, we would be content to make do with what was available.

But that wasn't what stymied me. The furnishings we did have didn't have a legitimate name, and rather than succumb to feeling ignorant and uninformed, I felt compelled to contrive an answer to this frequently asked question. I began to say we decorated in "Early Attic." It worked.

Oftentimes, I created my own mental pictures of the styles others specifically described as their individual choices. Of course, my "images" would have horrified interior decorators, but I was amused.

I never completely appreciated many styles—Louis Quatorze?—and several have remained enigmas to me. For awhile I even suspected anyone could market an idea simply by giving it an intriguing name.

Even though most style names were relatively simple, at that time a convincing-sounding salesperson could have told me Dark Ages Dungeon, Deliberately Depression, or Blitzkrieg Basic were legitimate trends.

Early American was one of the most popular styles, but even that was too broad for me to grasp. I immediately envisioned teepee-like houses with peace pipe towel bars and totem pole hat racks tastefully placed. Or, for the "other Early Americans," one-room log structures with walk-in fireplaces. The current interest in log houses may be a resurgence of that style with walk-in closets instead.

My favorite expression of all was "period pieces." It had a curious, almost mysterious ring to it. I have never figured out what periods were included, or if only knowledgeable people were able to identify the period by the pieces—fur rugs from the Cave Dweller Period—lava lawn chairs from the Vesuvian Period?

To the uninformed such as I, "period piece" was a vague but safe expression, something like "I'm not quite sure." I understood uncertainty. I kept it in mind for future reference.

Over time I discovered other people shared my sentiments about not having specifically named decors. As a result, they, too, invented styles in an effort to answer that often asked question. The names were as different as the individuals who created them, but the concept of being able to name the style remained important.

Besides our own Early Attic decor, I've heard cleverly personalized styles referred to as Early Available, Available Rejects, Old and Accessible, Attic Renaissance, No Strings or Springs Attached, Classic Charitable, Curbside Restoration, Top of the Line Good Will, Garage Sale Special, Recently Out of Style, Best of the Bargain Basement Line, Basementville, Previously Used and Abused, Great White Elephant, Pre-Inheritance, and even Dead Relative.

Perhaps eclectic decorating found its beginnings with graduates from the "School of Cheap" who gathered acquisitions frugally before unlimited credit became a recognized life style. Lack of ready cash to buy new matching furniture inspired a trend that eventually became a socially acceptable form of nose-thumbing at decorating purism.

I revived my thoughts about decorating schemes while leafing through a current publication promoting the splashiest, gaudiest, most mismatched display of colors, designs, and assorted furnishings I'd seen in a long time. In fact, the word "psychedelic" immediately came to mind as I suffered a mild wave of vertigo looking at the pages.

But then, melding differences is what eclectic is all about, mixing and matching to your heart's content. Perhaps the sixties is when eclectic officially began to be recognized, and it may be about to enjoy its first revival.

I wonder if these psychedelic furnishings are now considered "period pieces." I wonder, too, if our furniture finally qualifies as "period pieces." Any of those styles mentioned above would still apply, although "Old Junk Our Kids Refused to Take Off Our Hands for Free" is the way it's usually described.

I could start over and put all our current furniture out by the curb, but then I'd have to deal with a real embarrassment—its still being there after the rubbish truck made its rounds. That, or hearing what the neighbors would call it, which could be worse than not having a "proper" name for it.

"Period pieces," "eclectic," and "I'm not quite sure," are all somewhat synonymous to me, with only vague subtleties separating them. Any one would describe our belongings.

However, of the three phrases, "period pieces" still holds a certain amount of fascination for me, which is good. It's the most applicable since it emphasizes old things.

I'm simply going to change "Early Attic" to "The Attic Period." That sounds comfortable, and I like comfort any way I can get it.

CHICKEN SOUP SALVATION—FEBRUARY 13, 1996

Speaking of comfort, I have just finished reading *Chicken Soup for the Soul,* by Jack Canfield and Mark Victor Hansen. This book comes as close as possible to the comfort of the real thing without actually having to be cooked first. I highly recommend it to anyone. It takes only a couple of hours to read through it, but I have no doubt its worth will be measured over a much longer period.

The authors suggest the reader take time, read slowly, and let the collection of stories sink in. Initially, I didn't permit myself that luxury, however, as I moved along reading through the many selections, shedding an occasional tear (but more often smiling), I found myself slowing down and letting the words offer some meaning to me.

I know I've already gained measurably from the first reading, but in all likelihood, the comfort I felt from the messages contained therein will prompt me to return for repeated, more leisurely readings.

There is a sequel, a second helping as it were, of another 101 stories to which I have already treated myself. In many ways, these two books are like the real chicken soup. They offer temporary helpings of security in moments of turmoil, provide a comfortable buffer against the cold weather, offer much needed nourishment when I'm under the weather, or simply uplift my spirits when they've slipped.

And, just as I feel the need to digest as much soup as my body will hold in times of physical need, so, too, will I read as much as these two authors offer when in need of mental reassurance. It is important to have reliable sources for my chicken soup highs.

Naturally, after reading and making the correlation to chicken soup long enough, I began to feel the need to go into the kitchen and make the *real* thing. I could almost smell it simmering on the stove, creating an inviting and welcoming aroma throughout the house. The thoughts alone of the steaming elixir were causing my mouth to water. I *needed* to make a pot of chicken soup.

Unfortunately, I have a problem—I am incapable of performing this culinary feat satisfactorily. This shortcoming is more than disappointing. It's a major flaw in my role as chief cook and bottle washer (well, chief cook).

Whenever I make home made chicken soup, I dutifully chop, simmer, and stir. I even talk gently and encouragingly to it as I'm preparing the various ingredients. I fill it with flattery, saying how good it's going to taste and how everyone is going to love it. I give it special little pinches and tweeks of good foods and seasonings to enhance its flavor. I ladle it out . . . and it tastes like dish water!

What do I do wrong? How can I constantly ruin chicken soup? Yeah, yeah, I know, I get points for being consistent, but I need the soup, not credit for misplaced consistency. I need to know how to make the real thing as satisfying to my body as the books are to my mind.

I need to be able to approach this heart warming kitchen ritual confidently and emerge with something edible. No, more than edible, it has to be excellent enough to create the ultimate warm fuzzy feeling. Let's just say I'd like it to be so good a person would choose it over a double hot fudge sundae with all the trimmings. Now, *that* would be the quintessential chicken soup!

Thus far I've failed in my attempts, even after so many years of trying, and the only thing I'm convinced of is that no self-respecting chicken would want to be caught dead in my pot of soup. Well, no chicken is particularly happy about finding itself in anyone's pot, but it wouldn't want my soup to be its final resting place.

If I want to console anyone with chicken soup, it has to be doctored Campbell's; the doctoring largely consists of removing it from the can and offering it in a pretty tureen. Even though the thought is what counts, that thought would do little to comfort an ailing body or soul, unless that person has a good sense of humor and can feel restored through laughter.

I have a suggestion. No, I'm begging here, Folks. I need to know how to make a good pot of chicken soup, and there are so many of you who do it with such ease.

Do you share? Can you tell me the secret to success? I'd be forever grateful for your help. I'd like to be able to do more than read about it. I need to succeed at making the real thing.

Naturally, if it's a family secret, I'll respect your not wanting to share. After all, I do have Canfield's and Hansen's books, and will continue to get vicarious soup fixes through them, if necessary. Even repeated helpings of their written versions are better than anything I now produce on the stove. Believe me!

Read the book, please. It could make you understand my plight, bring out the good Samaritan in you, perhaps even make you feel sorry enough to save me from further embarrassment because I'm a chicken- soup- challenged cook!

A WOMAN FOR ALL SEASONS—JANUARY 7, 1997

William Safire once said, "Never assume the obvious is true." It's been an interesting challenge, but I finally have concluded that, obvious or not, many things simply are not always what they seem to be on the surface, and answers to questions are not necessarily always true or false, right or wrong, or good or bad.

I often wish we could rely more comfortably on things being as we perceive them. It would make life much simpler. More boring, perhaps, but easier in many ways.

I am reminded of a speaker at a workshop I once attended who addressed the concept of how differently people perceive what we often refer to as the simple, obvious "facts" in life. He gave a wonderful example of why, because of these differences in perception, simple answers to questions do not exist. He pointed out, among other things, how necessary it is to factor in who is being asked, where that person lives, and what main interests that person pursues, especially if that person is young. The example seemed obvious: "Name the four seasons?"

He informed us a young boy who lived in his part of the western United States might be very quick to answer, "deer, rabbit, squirrel, and duck!" and he'd be serious. Those who live in a climate with little, if any, variation, don't understand or appreciate why some of us use the weather or specific calendar months to define our seasons.

That same question asked of someone living in the northern Ohio area would elicit a totally different response, especially in light of the unseasonal weather we tend to experience regularly. The answers might not be what you expect, and they surely would be a bit tongue-in-cheek.

In response to what the four seasons are in Ohio, I have heard people say, "In which month?", or in some cases, "On which day?" Some people note Ohio's the only place they've ever visited (Thank God!) that has all four seasons in one day; wait a few minutes if you're unhappy with it, it will change soon. I have decided, however, that some years we may have five seasons.

As for what those five seasons might be called, most people probably would agree we have spring, summer, autumn, and winter, in no particular order and not necessarily in agreement with the calendar. I have added the fifth, which seems to come around every third or fourth day and is a combination of any of the above known seasons, often bearing no resemblance to the one it's supposed to be at that time of year. As yet, its name is "unprintable."

In recent years, fashion conscious women have gone through a period of equating themselves with seasons in a different, more personal way. The operative question making the rounds at female social gatherings was, "What season are you?" It was a given among those who were knowledgeable that the discussion was about correctly matching the colors a woman chooses for her wardrobe with the combined colors of her hair, eyes, and skin tone.

Here was a case where I definitely had been assuming the obvious, that a woman wears the colors she likes. Unfortunately, the only thing I ever learned from those who were wiser than I about these choices was that the colors I really like are the ones I shouldn't be wearing. To this day I still can't figure out why I'm winter! I probably should have invented a fifth season for satisfying my personal wardrobe choices, too. Perhaps I did and never named it.

Seasons are easily recognizable points of reference when discussing people's ages, too. If one uses an average life span of eighty years, it is generally assumed one is in the spring years until about the age of twenty, summer until forty, autumn until sixty, and winter thereafter.

If we remember the words of Safire, however, we'll assume no such thing. I'm sure most of us know a lot of people whose chronological ages clearly do not fit the assumed seasonal descriptions of those same ages. Like the season that identifies a person's wardrobe, the season that identifies a person's age also should not be assumed.

Places for taking vacations may have off-seasons, while some fruits are in-season only at certain times of the year. We have holiday seasons, baseball and football seasons, hunting seasons, and mating seasons. There is a "Man For All Seasons" (how come a man can be for all seasons, but a woman feels compelled to limit herself to just one?) What purpose do all these different definitions for seasons serve?

I don't know for sure, but regardless of what Safire says, I'm assuming I'll be dressed in the wrong colored clothing. I'm assuming I'll be looking for strawberries when, in fact, I should be looking for pumpkins. And I'm definitely assuming I'll act inappropriately for my age, no matter what I'm doing, what my age is, or what season it is.

However, like the speaker at the workshop, I'll never assume the obvious, that there are only four seasons.

SENIOR MOMENTS—MAY 12, 1998

Another season that isn't officially on a calendar but should be is the one when many of us begin to experience what my friend Julie calls "Senior Moments." I have seasons when I spend an inordinate amount of time trying to either analyze or talk my way out of a series of senior moments, so many, in fact, that if I could, I would walk away from myself for awhile, or at least try to turn a calendar page.

A "Senior Moment" is loosely defined as a brief interruption in sensible thinking and/or actions, a definition acknowledged by normally creditable people of maturity who have spent uncomfortable times extricating their feet from their mouths, or regretting the lack of an action that should have been a given.

"Senior Moments" are not fatal, although upon infrequent occasions such a consequence has seemed like the only acceptable solution that would exonerate me. No, the greatest side effect of "S.M.s" is a temporarily elevated level of stupidity, which I experience after marathon "S.M.ing", when I do things like introduce myself to someone I've known a long time.

In that particular instance I couldn't even beg off by saying the years had dulled my memory and/or eyesight because it had only been a few months since I'd seen her. The truth was glaringly obvious, and I drew a total blank.

"S.M.s," however, do not necessarily have to involve another party. It's highly possible to experience them alone. For example, more than once I've carried an object from room to room because I couldn't remember why I'd picked it up in the first place. Upon occasion I've accidentally been reminded of my mission when something else triggered the mechanism that shifts the mind back into gear.

Other times, when I've finally tired of carrying the thing, I've simply abandoned it en route to somewhere else. When I eventually come across it again, I'm puzzled to find it in a strange location; misplaced objects defy explanation.

Some of my more private "S.M.s" could remain just that, private. No one has to know I once started to drain the spaghetti before I put the colander into the sink, or that I "lost" a slice of toast that literally flew out of the toaster and hid behind the appliance, but huggermuggery is not my way to deal with brief episodes of mental shut-down.

Networking has been my life line to maintaining sanity. I've found immense relief, and a link to normalcy, in learning my peers often were in the throes of similar dilemmas as I at various ages and stages of life:

▪ Discovering, after much pleading to get permission to wear them, that other young girls preferred the comfort of sneakers to fashionably adult heels and hose.

▪ Hearing other seemingly assured new mothers often felt as lost and overwhelmed as I about all the new responsibilities of parenthood.

▪ Sighing with enormous relief upon learning other, more poised and composed-looking new teachers were equally as frightened as I the first days in a classroom.

"Senior Moments" are merely advanced stages of what I think of as ongoing phases—Teen Tribulations, Parent Pathos, or Adult Anxieties. The immeasurable reassurance gained by knowing others confront the same trying moments is an important reminder of our humanness.

It's really okay not to know everything all the time. Even the biggest, most sophisticated computer systems in the world experience periodic, temporary malfunctions, but they don't have the luxury of excusing them as "Senior Moments."

I know my retrieval system will occasionally be down, but the brief lapses aren't permanent. The human mind is the most unique, state-of-the-art computer in creation, but even it is not perfect. Thankfully, it gets to enjoy the indulgence of communicating with other human minds to compare methods for dealing with the imperfections.

Computers communicate with each other, but they can't feel the experience, nor can they understand the thrill of recovering from a "Senior Moment," or any other awkward situation.

A GAP THAT WON'T BE BRIDGED—MARCH 29, 1993

Occasionally it takes a little while to laugh at myself, especially when I find myself in dilemmas such as:

"Three no trump."

"Pass."

"Pass."

"Pass."

"Oh, no!"

Instead, it's time to panic, at least temporarily, since I'm never quite sure how or why I got to this point in the bidding and am faced with having to do something now that it's stopped with me. It strikes terror into my heart.

I have been playing at the game of bridge forever; Charles and Omar would no doubt suggest I not admit that in public. But the mechanism governing my improvement is definitely, irreparably broken when it involves this game. I can apply my intelligence to a wide variety of subjects, but bridge is not one of them. Knowing the rules is one thing; remembering what to do with them is quite another.

As a result, the ladies with whom I play are forced to test their patience and tolerance on a regular basis. Will this be the evening I remember what "double" means: that I do or do not have to bid? At what point in the bidding is one no trump indicative of a high or a low count? Is it possible I'll make it through the entire evening without having to ask for help from someone at the other table? *Not!*

Many people believe once we've learned something it is stored permanently in the memory bank, and while it is sometimes difficult to retrieve, it will return, a little like that bike riding business.

I think this is no doubt true, but one has to learn it well first, and I know I have never fully and credibly learned how to play bridge. I'm like the swimmer who never ventures into water deep enough to prevent his feet from touching the bottom while his head sticks out of the water. He sort of swims, as I sort of play bridge. For people who are tournament-caliber bridge players, who still remember four hands (or four weeks) later when and why they played each card, I present a real challenge in practicing patience.

Honest, I attempt to pre-think several plays in order to make the transportation work, for example. I then proceed to misplay the first trick in the series, throw off the entire sequence, and don't make the bid. I recognize my mistake right after the first card is down. It won't work because I'm on the wrong side of the board. I feel *Duh* should be written in large, red letters across my forehead.

There are some things on which I can concentrate intently for hours, but I struggle to remember if there is yet one more trump card out against me. You can only imagine my turmoil when playing a no trump bid. Do I remember every card in every suit? Do you honestly believe pigs can fly?

The entire process defies analysis. I *know* what to do, and before each meeting I swear I'm going to concentrate and think ahead. There is no excuse for my wandering mind. I mentally vow I won't lead a suit that was mentioned in the bidding by the opponents (unless I suspect my partner has none, but I'm never right about that one). I'll try to bid aggressively if I have a bridge-lover's hand, but keep my mouth shut if it is a marginal nightmare. Underbidding, overbidding, not making the bid— the things I do best!

I am convinced somewhere in my circuitry there's a flaw, and each time I approach this game and have to direct my thinking toward it, I see the sign: BRIDGE OUT AHEAD.

Do I heed the warning? Of course not. I forge ahead boldly, optimistically thinking I can somehow vault the distance between failure and success, thereby closing this gap once and for all. This achievement has continued to escape me, and as a result, I wind up treading water somewhere in between, hoping to make it to the opposite side of the evening before I lose completely and drown.

Maybe the hardest thing to understand is I keep playing. In fact, that may seem to be the dumbest thing I have to own up to, but I am not ready to admit the distribution and manipulation of fifty-two cards can be outside my realm of intelligence.

There is more than simply trying to master the art of a particular card game involved here, however. The fellowship and camaraderie that result from time shared with good friends override my apparent lack of ability to remember all those rules. They make me the winner every time, regardless of how I play the game.

They are so long-suffering.

Two Scoops of Common Sense—April 27, 1992

I admit to being a borderline bridge player. I also recognize my limited understanding of how the economy works. What is really happening when all those people are shouting and telephoning at the stock exchange, and why is spending a lot of money the key, according to some, to getting the country out of a recession?

I may not have the mind of an economist, but, really, I do have common sense, and I have some serious questions about the way our free enterprise system works. My mind doesn't grasp figures that run beyond six places, so I'll avoid the government's budget deficit of kabillions of dollars and speak from the position of an average consumer.

The advertisers' claims about what they are offering the public, and what the people really get, is an area to which I relate well. Are we as gullible as we sometimes appear to be?

Let's begin by discussing something very basic and common. When I go into the supermarket to purchase coffee, I find I am paying the same or more for a thirteen ounce can as I used to pay for a sixteen ounce can. Pardon me, but I would like the full sixteen ounces, not thirteen. I do not fully understand how they arrived at this odd amount at all, but that is not the significant issue here.

Some admen have launched a campaign to convince us, the consumers, we get just as many cups per thirteen ounce can as we got from a sixteen ounce can. Personally, I disagree, but if they want to sell the coffee only in odd-sized increments, why don't they just do it?

Because they can't. If they did, they would have to sell it for less, a compromise they obviously choose not to make. We get three ounces less but still pay as much or more than we did for the full pound. Am I missing something here?

Or, how about this peculiar logic. In the interest of eating more nutritiously, manufacturers remove the supposedly bad ingredients from food, then proceed to charge us more for the finished product. Its counterpart, which still contains all the original contents, is sitting beside it on the shelf for less money.

The less we get, the more we pay for it. Take out the sodium, increase the price; remove the fat, increase the price; eliminate the cholesterol, increase the price. I have no doubt it costs money to process these foods, but I do question the amounts we seem to be paying for this service. Perhaps I should be thankful there are those who are concerned with the public's health and well-being, but that concern leaves me with more than a few unanswered questions.

Every time I see an ad on television for a certain cereal that has two scoops of raisins, common sense again surfaces and creates confusion in my mind. The manufacturer clearly wants me to become excited because it sounds like such a great quantity when they promote the product. *I want to know the size of the scoop!*

I have a set of measuring tools shaped like scoops; therefore, to me, the cereal makers could be using any size from one-fourth of a teaspoon to one cup of raisins.

My better judgement suggests it isn't either of these two extremes, but I still don't know how much it is. Are they the size of those little plastic dispensers that come in powdered drink cannisters, or perhaps the size of an ice cream scoop? I checked every chart of weights and measurements I could find and nowhere was there a definition of a scoop. A pinch, yes, but no scoops.

And another thing (pardon me, Mary Lou). While on the subject of two scoops, do they intend for us to understand they put in two of the same sized scoops, no matter what the size of the box? The ten-ounce box gets the same two scoops as the twenty-five ounce box? My suspicions give way to out and out distrust about believing the statement "truth in advertising." If it's bent, is it still truthful?

Common sense is so much a part of our decision-making process. Why do we allow ourselves to be easily led into accepting what advertisers want us to believe? We seem to do it all the time, perhaps because it's easier than concerning ourselves with defining "truths"—all's fair in love and war . . . and advertising?

Many years ago, as a kid, I learned a card trick from a friend of my parents. It was terribly simple, really, but I thought it was terrific and delighted in showing it to my own friends. In retrospect, I realized it was a lesson in getting others to believe what I wanted them to believe.

They didn't suspect immediately that I was controlling their responses. When repeated several times, of course, they usually were able to figure out how I was manipulating their words in order to make the trick work. It was in fun, but it demonstrated how easily we can be duped with words.

I will continue to buy thirteen instead of sixteen-ounce cans of coffee, and it won't matter what size the scoops are. I will continue to eat the cereal anyway—I haven't begun to actually count the raisins . . . yet!

It isn't right or even honest, but then, no one ever said life is fair. This is one more example of how the real world looks without the rose-tinted glasses of innocence.

But then, when is the last time you saw a knight in shining armor?

SOME QUESTIONS HAVE NO ANSWERS
—JANUARY 9,1996

With the help of the five most commonly recognized question words—who, what, where, when, and why—it's easy to ask a lot of questions. Getting answers to those questions, however, is not always simple. If anything, they often scratch the surface and lead to more questions.

A piece of mail that arrived one day prompted one

of those curious situations. It was from a well-known magazine, informing us on the envelope that a treasurer's advisory notice was enclosed. We opened it with an appropriate tongue-in cheek amount of oohing and aahing before disposing of the "you-could-be-a-winner" notice.

Of course, we hadn't won anything, but hope remains eternal. The puzzler was how we'd become eligible for another final stage when we hadn't returned anything from previous mailings. If we had the sum of money generated in sending all the "get-your-hopes-up" mail we've received over the years, we'd be able to buy a year's supply of soft cones from McDonald's, and for us, that's a lot of soft cones!

It would be refreshing to satisfy all the aspects of a situation once in awhile, but it doesn't work that way. For example, I always experience this conflict during the Ohio State-Penn State football game.

I'm a native born Ohioan, support Ohio teams, and want them to win. Unfortunately, I don't like Ohio State's coach. On the other hand, I have a great deal of respect for Penn State's coach, Joe Paterno, so I am immediately caught on the horns of a dilemma; I want the Buckeyes to win but don't want Paterno to lose. I still haven't figured out a satisfactory solution to give this problem a happy ending.

Years ago a person much wiser than I shared a thought provoking statement: Since we have two eyes, two ears, but only one mouth, we might learn more by looking and listening twice as much as talking. It's good advice up to a point, but it neglects to stress the importance of asking questions when satisfactory answers are not forthcoming.

Nowadays, many things I see and hear are educated

opinions, which often lead to more questions, sort of a Catch-22 situation. Instead of solutions, I have variables. Now, not all questions create dilemmas for me, but some issues do pique my curiosity more than others. High on my own list of perplexities are the (maybe unanswerable) questions surrounding Superman. For openers, why a phone booth? The thing is barely big enough to change your mind much less your clothes. One always just happens to be handy, but they are so exposed. He may be "faster than a speeding bullet," but, come on, no one ever sees him entering as Clark Kent and exiting as Superman? If he's needed in a modern-day mall, how does C.K. transform into the Big S, where phone "booths" are nothing but walk-up counters in the aisles?

And this whole disguise thing. Like, glasses really change a person's appearance that much. Even as a young child I suspected Lois Lane was the one who needed glasses but was too vain to wear them in public. If she has finally succumbed to wearing contacts, they must be in upside down.

Her years of myopic ignorance regarding her co-worker belies her credibility as a keen-eyed reporter. How can we be expected to believe neither she, Jimmy, nor Perry have ever seen Clark without his glasses, or can't figure out the timeliness of his disappearances? Paging Sherlock Holmes.

While I'm on the subject of the enigmatic Clark Kent/ Superman, how many changes of that designer red and blue underwear does the man own? Obviously, he wears it constantly, and no one backs away because he's "offensive." It must have been tough keeping outfits clean before automatic washers, dryers, and permanent press fabrics.

That cape is the real mind-boggler to me, though. How does he get it so neatly folded and tucked up under his shirt so quickly? Why isn't there an unsightly bulge between his shoulder blades? With six yards of material shoved under his shirt he should resemble the Hunchback of Notre Dame!

I've asked these stupid questions almost since Superman was born (or whatever... that just leads to more unanswered questions), and I've finally decided my acceptance of this mythical character, along with some other curious oddities, is an example of how much I still need and want to believe in heroes and happy endings.

Perhaps I overlook some obvious impossibilities because it's easier to remain positive and hopeful without explanations for everything. Apparently, I can accept some things without knowing why.

Then again, maybe these situations serve to remind me that life doesn't always offer easy solutions to puzzling questions but rather is an ongoing mystery I feel compelled to try to solve from time to time.

Or, maybe there really aren't any simple answers. Superman and the possibility of winning something just help to keep our hopes up and intact.

Which reminds me, I have to buy a lottery ticket.

ASK A SILLY QUESTION—FEBRUARY 7, 1997

"Do you want the windows painted opened or shut?"

More than twenty years ago my husband asked that absurd question from atop a ladder propped outside the kitchen window. As silly as it was, it sent my visiting friend, Donna, and me into ripples of laughter. Levity is such a wonderful way to get through mundane, unpleasant tasks.

We met Donna and her husband quite by accident one evening after many years of not having seen each other. We had dinner together and all laughed again as we remembered that never-to-be-forgotten, ridiculous question.

It was but one of the fond memories we shared, and just one example of how strong long time friendships can be. We sat and talked as though we'd been together just a week before. We covered everything from past and current work problems we'd shared to new highlights in our respective lives, including her new status as a grandmother.

It was such a silly question that triggered so many memories, but then, there are many of those every day. Some have obvious answers, but the question I stumble over the most comes after an encounter like our recent one with Donna: "Where have so many years gone in such a short time?" I had to remind myself she and I met and began working together almost thirty years ago.

As a result of this chance meeting, the window painting question made me think about how many decisions, serious and otherwise, I've made recently.

Would I make the same choices again if given the opportunity to try again? How much have I learned from the decisions I have made in all those years? When do you know if you've made the best decision possible? Is it true that the more you learn the less you know? Incidentally, are any of these questions even important?

Having more questions than answers disturbs me. It isn't neatly balanced, and I want to have balance and orderliness.

I considered several possible questions I, and others like me, confront on any given day, questions that offer me the definite opportunity to make decisions, express opinions, and keep the question-answer ratio equal.

At the grocery store I'm always asked to decide between paper or plastic bags.

When I buy a lottery ticket, the cashier optimistically asks me if I want cash or installments.

In a restaurant I get asked to make several choices, for example:

Which do you prefer, smoking or non?

A table or a booth?

What can I get you to drink?

Do you want a baked Idaho or a baked sweet potato?

What two vegetables would you like with your dinner?

Would you care for soup or salad?

How would you like your meat cooked?

Is everything okay?

More coffee?

Have you saved room for dessert?

Can I get you anything else this evening?

Apparently, I do make decisions more often than I realized, and the scales are kept fairly well balanced, but I still came back to the original question: did I want the windows painted opened or shut.

It's ridiculous, of course, and I'll no doubt always remember that question, but I've forgotten the answer. I suspect we were laughing so hard I never did answer it. Perhaps always having definite answers to everything and keeping things in proportion isn't nearly as important as I sometimes want to make it.

Donna was the one who brought up that absurd question when we met for dinner that evening. It once again amused us and set us laughing.

She didn't remember whether we decided to have the windows painted opened or closed, either, but we all remembered the amusement and laughter we got to share so often over the many years of this long standing friendship, all because of that silly question.

I still don't know where all those years have gone in such a short time, but it doesn't matter very much. The friendship that resulted from those years is what counts.

Really demonstrates what's important, doesn't it?

How Old Is Your Maytag?—April 4, 1995

My friend Julie has an avocado Maytag.

"Doesn't everyone?" she asked as she wrapped hers around her and fastened up the front.

For Julie, the symbolic analogy to something out of the past (avocado has been out of vogue for years) that remains serviceable indefinitely (Maytags last almost forever) is a puffy, durable winter jacket purchased many frigid seasons ago. It may not be her choice for daily outdoor winter wear, but when the winds become blustery and the mercury goes south on the thermometer, out it comes. It is still respectable looking and reliably warm!

Stop a moment to think about it. You probably have at least one Maytag, an item that withstands any tough treatment directed its way, shows little or no wear in spite of hundreds of cleanings, and always comes through dependably when nothing else measures up to the occasion.

An avocado Maytag is a "take-for-granted" item. Because of its steadfastness, parting with it would be an act of betrayal to its years of loyalty, and is rarely a consideration.

On the heels of her comment, I realized I had several relics of my own. Among them is a pair of new-looking spectator pumps I keep hoping will come back in style, although I'd no doubt break something vital (or at least suffer nosebleeds) if I ever wore such high heels again.

And there's the old enamel canner I know would perform well if I chose to press it into service again, even though it has already bathed thousands of cans of fruits and vegetables.

But perhaps my most obvious avocado Maytag is a raincoat. Make that "was" a raincoat.

It was a dark brown and black plaid, straight-lined, simply tailored in a gabardine-like fabric, and could be worn even if it wasn't raining. I'd had it at least ten, maybe twelve years, always felt comfortable in it, and never thought about getting rid of it until friends (and my mother) began kidding me.

"You *still* have that old coat?" "Hasn't that thing worn out *yet?*" "Aren't you just plain *tired* of it?" Or, more to the point, "When are you going to *get rid* of that thing?"

I never thought of it as being out of date. It was too basic a style, and the fabric wore like iron. Until the kidding, I hadn't entertained any notions about replacing it. It was serving me so well I never thought much of anything about it, I merely took it for granted.

Unfortunately, after enough teasing, I began to experience moments of doubt each time I got it out of the closet. Perhaps it was time for a new raincoat. My doubts gradually gave way to more serious considerations, which in turn gave way to action.

I carefully, almost tenderly, folded and added the coat to the collection of items going to the Good Will Center. It was more than a little difficult—that feeling of betrayal nagged in the back of my mind—but I kept repeating to myself that it was time, it was time.

That momentous decision, when the raincoat I have became the raincoat I had, was more than ten years ago, and in those years I have been unable to find another one with which I've been satisfied.

I've tried to replace my good old standby with long clear things, short plastic things, belted Columbo-like things, flowing tent-like things, hooded things, shiny, colorful, artificial-fabric things, fold-up-into-little-envelopes things, and they're all still just that: THINGS! I want my serviceable, reliable, comfortable, raincoat back!

Somewhere out there, a woman about my size is wearing a coat that belonged to me. I know it's still around — it will never wear out. I gave up my right to it in a weak moment of succumbing to peer pressure (shame on me!) and have regretted it ever since.

My coat symbolized an old Maytag. Perhaps I was subconsciously embarrassed into thinking I should feel more compassion for the poor bored serviceman. Maybe I just wanted him to have something more of a life, and if I parted with my old reliable coat that never required anything of me, I somehow might be symbolically providing him with an opportunity to do something.

Of course it's a lousy analogy, but there was no good excuse for giving away something perfectly good just because others thought it was time I did so.

I needed some reason to make myself feel better. I should have sent the guy homemade cookies to make him feel better instead.

I'm issuing a warning. If ever you are out in public wearing *my coat,* and an unfamiliar, excited woman races toward you, gesturing wildly and yelling words that even vaguely resemble "my'" and "coat," be on guard. I'll negotiate first, but I make no promises if you refuse to consider my offer. I'm desperate.

(Sigh) "If it ain't broke. . . ."

A PERSONAL PERSPECTIVE ON BIRDS
—OCTOBER 9, 1993

Normally, I'm calm and objective about things, but I do tend to have strong opinions; some I express and others I just ponder over. As I was taking down the hummingbird feeder for the season, I found myself reviewing the impressions I have developed about birds over the years.

True bird watchers are dedicated to the appreciation of the species, and are able to identify several varieties by such details as seasonal colors, sizes, markings, and songs. I admire this but am totally incapable of doing it.

I enjoy watching birds, but will never qualify as a genuine bird watcher. For one thing, I can't always detect details like the color of the wing bars, or for that matter, if there are wing bars. I'm okay with the really obvious ones like bright red cardinals or hummingbirds (am I good or what?) but for the most part birds move too fast for me to check their credentials.

Nevertheless, I do observe them and have drawn some general conclusions about their roles. For example, those cardinals are truly beautiful creatures, but they know it so they tend to pose a lot in places where people will appropriately ooh and aah over them.

The blue jays, on the other hand, are the bullies of the bird community, which completely overrides and diminishes their outer beauty. Whatever they want they take, using their size to intimidate smaller birds. I often wonder if their bravado extends to confrontations with large birds.

Since our hummingbird feeder hangs right outside the window, I've been privy to their habits at close range. For such tiny creatures they possess an incredible amount of speed and energy matched by a fiercely tenacious defensive quality necessary for survival. However, most disturbing to me are the physical attacks on each other, the apparent unwillingness to share, as though they must claim and guard every food source as personal and private property.

Then there are the woodpeckers, the noisy, nervous ones who walk up and down tree trunks constantly banging their little beaks against the hard wood in search of insects. What a way to secure food. My head hurts just watching them. They must have an unlimited internal supply of Excedrin constantly being pumped into their systems.

In contrast, mourning doves are so calm and placid. The owl may be the recognized symbol of wisdom, but those doves are no dummies. They let the other birds jockey for position at the feeders while they patiently wait below, catching the large quantity of seeds the other birds carelessly shove to the ground. It's a catering service, with meals for which they've had to do almost no work, being delivered to them.

Speaking of work, the wrens appear to have an enormous capacity for it. Not only are their tiny bodies capable of rapidly building elaborate, structurally-sound nests (overnight, in our hanging baskets, thank you), but they also house powerful voices that are disproportionate to their tiny framework. How something so small can produce such big, beautiful results must be admired and enjoyed.

Not at all enjoyable are those big raucous crows. They meet as if in session, making a great deal of empty noise, constantly making their presence known. Might they be considered the politicians in the bird society?

My personal favorites are the chickadees. They're cute but never deliberately flaunt it. They get along well with most other birds, and are not greedy or nasty. They play! They spend their time in each other's company, flitting from tree to tree engaged in a game of tag, chirping in laughter-like tones.

Or they might half-seriously check out the bug population along a window frame, and occasionally peek in the window as they do so. They're more trusting than many birds; merely opening the door will not necessarily send them skittering away. Life, to them, is to be enjoyed from day to day—they're happy!

I can't describe the details about physical markings, but I do identify human-like characteristics in birds I see.

Perhaps all animal groups present similar images, but in birds I see: the peacekeepers and the trouble-makers; the industrious, hard working ones as well as those who always seek an easy way to do everything; the protectors and the aggressors; the friendly, sharing individuals along with the greedy, selfish ones; those with surface beauty and those whose beauty comes from within; and those to be trusted as well those to avoid.

Like humans, it takes all kinds to make up the whole of their world. Often, these observations and conclusions help me understand the coexistence of all creatures.

My version of bird watching is matching up the similarities between birds and people. Perhaps it isn't too unusual that I can readily identify so many of the same characteristics and qualities in both species. I've met some pretty strange birds who just happen to be people.

LOVE/HATE RELATIONSHIPS—FEBRUARY 1, 1998

Identifying interpretations of phrases isn't necessarily as consistent as matching birds to people. For instance, the term "love/hate relationship" might bring to mind lovers engaged in the trials and tribulations of a struggling affair.

However, time, experience, and observations on life from a different perspective have shown me how these strong opposing emotions can be related to much less dramatic circumstances. The implications of this contrary-sounding expression can be quite far-reaching.

I love new fresh snow at the beginning of winter, but I am quickly reminded of how ugly I feel towards the dirty stuff after five months of trudging everywhere blanketed under multiple layers of socks and sweaters, or white-knuckle driving in hazardous traffic conditions. To me, that's an obvious interpretation of a love/hate relationship.

The list of events that easily fit into this category goes on.

I love the brilliant richness of the leaves in autumn as they turn red, gold, and orange. Nothing is more glorious than a sunny October day when the leaves have reached the height of their magnificent burst of color. Then they turn brown, dry and shrivel up, fall to the ground, and need to be raked. I hate raking leaves.

There must be others who love planning and planting gardens only to have that passion transformed to hatred when they discover they can't eliminate the invasion of weeds, insects, and any other vermin that have greater stamina and resources in the war between the species.

At one time I seriously loved and looked forward to putting in a garden, spurred on by the mid-winter arrival of mail catalogs displaying inviting pictures of lush, vine-ripened tomatoes, pumpkins that could only be transported by wheel barrow, and roses, Oh, yes, delicate, prize winning, velvety blooms in jewel-like tones.

Those photographs never showed anyone trying to remove weeds the size of Rhode Island, aphids that welcomed any pesticides as though they were elixirs, or woodchucks and raccoons that remained undaunted as they laid claim to any and all of my produce. I loved the catalog pictures. I hated trying to stave off the forces that kept me from achieving anything even remotely close to resembling them.

Inside the home, right near the top of my personal list of love/hate relationship examples, are fitted sheets.

I love the way they fit so snugly and smoothly on the bed, stay tucked in, and remain relatively unrumpled.

I hate putting them on the beds.

Fitted sheets have no doubt contributed to more broken finger nails, not to mention broken or at least sprained fingers, than any other household threat.

Unfortunately, there's a direct correlation between how securely and tightly they fit and the amount of tugging and stretching involved to get them into place properly. At various times in this struggle, I've been convinced I was attempting to fit a twin-sized sheet on a double-sized bed because there was no way the amount of sheet I had was going to cover the bed on which I was trying to put it.

Aside from the physical stamina required to stretch

them over a mattress, there is the mental challenge of figuring out how to refold them.

New sheets in unopened packages create the optical illusion of being neatly and flatly folded; they are neither, a fact that becomes painfully obvious once they're released from the sealed wrapping. It's because of these ornery, uncooperative, poorly refolded "lumps" of material linen closets have been given a bad name. I finally solved this frustrating exercise in futility by not even trying. I wrestle the sheets from the beds, launder, then struggle with them to remake the beds. My family used to praise my timing if they were still warm and it was bedtime, unless, of course, it happened to be August. I'm serious about this exercise, if I had ever succeeded in neatly folding a contour sheet, I never would have unfolded it again.

There are many ways to interpret love/hate relationships (more than I want to know), and dirty snow, crummy leaves, weed-filled gardens, and sheets that appear to defy the laws of physics only scratch the surface.

The concept these relationships represent is an old one that has been expressed in many different forms, explaining one of life's most basic lessons:

- Learning to take the bitter with the better.
- No pain, no gain.
- Into each life a little rain must fall.
- To have rainbows, we must have rain.
- And my personal favorite: No one ever said it was going to be easy.

It would be unique if everything in life was simple, remained beautifully unchanged, and never presented a challenge; but then, perhaps we'd never understand that "easy doesn't do it."

After all, if we never faced ugliness, would we ever learn how to appreciate beauty? Better still, would we even recognize it?

THE END OF THE STARTER—September 19, 1995

I've concluded yeast starters are not among the beautiful things in life. Our daughter offered me hers after she'd dealt with all that bubbling and brewing long enough. It can be a real nuisance, but I couldn't see intentionally destroying it, so I accepted it. Dumb idea!

If you aren't familiar with starters, consider yourself fortunate, but I don't understand how you've managed to escape them. Either your friends think too much of you to foist one of these bubbly brews on to you, or you have intelligent friends who avoid confrontations with things that ferment.

This is my third venture into growing edible cultures. You'd think I'd learn, wouldn't you? They've all been different. They've all been demanding. They've all been like something out of a Stephen King novel.

The first was a combination of fruits, the second a sourdough batter, and now this one, a batter for Amish Cinnamon Cake. The purpose of having one of these conglomerations is to advance it to the appropriate fermented stage, after which you add the growing substance to other recognizable ingredients and eat it.

These starters control people who keep them. They are cyclical, usually coming full circle on schedules ranging between ten days and two weeks. After that, you get to perform each day's duty all over again. This necessitates keeping a calendar on which you mark the specific activity assigned to its designated day.

You might be required simply to stir the contents, or

maybe add a certain combination of ingredients. There are even days when you do nothing, but the point is the order in which you stir, add, or do nothing is critical to the proper fermentation process.

Finally, on the last day of each cycle, you are expected to bake something, after you've divided, conquered, and shared the bounty. It is imperative you have a long list of friends because you only get to share a batch with each person once; otherwise, you create a long list of enemies!

It was late on a Saturday night when I brought this latest batch of frothy-looking liquid paste back from a visit with our daughter, so before going to bed I instinctively put it into the refrigerator without even glancing at the sheet of instructions. After all, it contained milk, therefore, it should be kept chilled.

The following morning I reviewed my instructions for day number two (which was actually day nine in the cycle), and just happened to notice, in rather large letters at the bottom of the page, NEVER REFRIGERATE. Oops!

I immediately removed it from the refrigerator, but had no way of knowing whether or not it was still alive. I was to stir that day, add to and divide the next, and finally bake Tuesday. I felt I had little choice but to play it out.

Another potentially embarrassing problem was that in sharing the divided portions of this particular batch, I might wind up giving dead glop to a friend. It was important to choose someone who'd be very understanding!

And who would understand this conditional offering better than my neighbor Mary Beth! I knew I could give her this questionable substance secure in the knowledge she could do with it whatever she pleased, or nothing if she didn't please, and wouldn't have to worry about pleasing me.

I hoped that in the exchange process I emphasized enough that the mixture would be compatible with the garbage disposal. In fact, it might even be beneficial to the functioning of the septic system if she decided not to cater to the daily needs and demands of the slowly bubbling brew.

I don't especially enjoy being on call to cater to a container of questionable contents, but I'm incapable of throwing away anything in any way associated with food. It must be the guilt we felt if we wasted food when others were hungry and starving in Europe during World War II. However, after a short time of looking at this gruel-like concoction, I decided even hungry children might opt for beetles. This is ugly stuff! Nevertheless, I proceeded on schedule.

Somewhere in the middle of all this monkey business, I called our daughter and asked if she had any idea what the death rate was on abused starters. She seemed to think it couldn't be killed off easily. Apparently she'd tried. I was having second thoughts about saving starters!

The countdown reached zero and I added what seemed like sixty-five ingredients necessary to transform this ugly substance into a beautiful cake. Soon, the inviting, heady aroma of cinnamon filled the house, the cake rose high, and even the color became appealing. I hadn't done it in after all.

I was relieved and my confidence was restored by my good fortune. I hadn't failed. I hadn't put an end to the starter before it had had a chance to reproduce at least once. Clearly this was success, but I'm no dummy.

I recognize when I've had as much of a good thing as my nerves will handle. I decided to quit while I was still ahead.

The next Amish Cinnamon Cake came from Holmes County.

Sometimes You'd Better Not Eat Your Wheaties
—September 8, 1992

If you are easily offended by an occasional colorful phrase, perhaps this story is not for you. If, on the other hand, you find it necessary, even helpful, to resort to expressive language every so often, you will no doubt share and understand the sentiments expressed around our place on a particularly troublesome day.

I personally know of no one who has never experienced a truly rotten day (week? month?) at some time or another in his or her life, but if you are so fortunate, then you might not fully appreciate the events of our consternation.

The offending day came at the end of an entire week of unpleasant hints of things to come, the kinds of things we ordinarily ignore because they appear to be insignificant. The first mistake was getting out of bed that particular morning to respond to a crack-of-dawn phone call. From there, things went straight downhill at a rapid clip. My husband was the object of all this compounded distress.

The first half of the day had been filled with everything Murphy could throw his way. There were several phone calls trying to persuade service companies we really needed service. These were followed by one company actually sending its representative a day ahead of schedule. The phone kept ringing, callers who were and were not related to the issues at hand, but who simply added to the confusion of a stressed person attempting to work through problems.

The frosting on this miserable cake was a sinus infection that had been building all week, causing nearly total lack of sleep, and finally creating a head that felt like a solid, concrete block. In short, nothing was right!

About midday yet another phone call came in, and when a thoroughly frustrated voice barked its hello, the familiar, friendly, understanding voice at the other end of the line simply said, "Whatsa matter, Dad, somebody pee in your Wheaties this morning?"

Disgusting? Distasteful? (no pun intended, honest!) Crude? Gross? Yes, to all of the above, and all my husband could do was laugh. What a fantastic sound! Of course, it wasn't going to magically make all the aggravation that had been building simply disappear, but it was the best tension-breaking comment he could have heard at that moment.

How often the most absurd, ridiculous little statement or action pulls us out of the pits, enough so we can regroup and marshal our forces to move on.

For most of us there are those situations, infrequent, we would hope, that are bigger than we are. Generally, we go along dealing with issues and concerns as they come at us, fielding things pretty well, not even stopping too long to think about our actions. It is merely a case of reacting on a regular basis to whatever life dishes out.

But then there's that moment of log jam, caused by the slightest incident, and everything seems to deteriorate rapidly. The handle slips away from us temporarily, and recapturing it becomes more difficult than "gathering feathers in a windstorm."

The replacement of a two-year-old boiler because of an approaching new gasline, a limping truck, a comatose tractor, the damaging invasion of a storage barn by brazen woodchucks, rapidly growing grass demanding attention whenever the rain stops long enough, unavailable service, a need to be in another city two hours away, and a sick body were simply too much for one morning.

There is no place to run and hide, although that always sounds like the perfect solution to any problem. And we cannot literally avoid getting out of bed; even if we could, we only would be prolonging the pain of confrontation.

It would be wonderful if we had some legitimate places to lay the blame for all the misfortunes that come our way, but since places like that can't be manufactured, we cannot shift the solutions to these issues elsewhere.

Probably the most difficult part is trying to figure out why all these things happen when there seems to be no justifiable cause for them. When our heads are clearer, however, it serves to remind us how little control we actually have over so many things in our lives. (How's that for a sobering thought?!) If nothing else, it should give us a greater resolve to manage well the things we *can* control.

Perhaps the offbeat type of humor is not the answer to all the ills of the world, but if it serves you just one time, it is more than worth it.

I'm quite sure it was never intended to be interpreted verbatim, but just to be on the safe side, the next time you sense a nasty rotten day on the horizon, get out of bed, get dressed, bypass the cereal cupboard, get into your car, head for the closest restaurant, and order a waffle.

PART IV

Carrying My Own Baggage

...

THEIR GRASS JUST LOOKED GREENER
—APRIL 30, 1996

When I was a little kid in grade school my appearance was not paramount in my thoughts. I was a confirmed tomboy, so my mother saw to it I was bathed daily, wore clean clothes, and had my hair neatly braided before I left for school in the morning. On Sundays, she patiently rolled my hair into fat, sausage-like curls. I exerted little, if any, effort towards the betterment of my appearance. It was a wonderful, literally care-free time in my life.

When I entered junior high school, life as I had known it abruptly changed. I became conscious of the fact my body was something more than a baseball-playing machine fueled by food at regular intervals.

I'm not sure when or how this change occurred. Again, like Topsy, maybe I just "growed," but suddenly, I had two ambitious goals: to wear my hair in a page boy style, and to acquire a flat tummy. Until then, I wasn't even aware I had an appearance, but there I was, attempting to rearrange as yet undeveloped proportions, and to organize my hair.

Regardless of how hard I tried to make it so, my hair was not meant to be fashioned in the desired style. I was born with curly hair but had tired of people clucking over my locks; I wasn't blond, but those compliments made me feel like Goldilocks. I was grown up and wanted to look the part. Sadly, my success was not immediately attainable.

Each day during lunch my friends and I exchanged important, newly-discovered information about developing shapely figures (ours were as yet undefined), clothes that made bold fashion statements (our wardrobes only whispered), creative application of make-up (which none of us were allowed to wear), and glamorous hair styles (ours were at best functional). These midday sessions prompted me to establish the tummy flattening goal.

I never had viewed myself sideways in a mirror before this startling revelation, but suddenly, that was the *only* way I approached one. I concluded I needed a girdle!

I found an old one of my mother's and asked permission to wear it. In her infinite wisdom, she did not point out the many shortcomings of my choice. She knew this was a lesson I would do well to learn on my own.

Soon after leaving home that momentous day with my reshaped torso, I learned merely *wearing* a girdle did not solve figure flaws. A girdle detail about which I had been innocently unaware (and had therefore overlooked), was that I had chosen an "open bottom style" meant to be held in place by attaching garters to hosiery which of course, I wasn't wearing.

Instead of solving one problem, I had quickly compounded it into three: I had acquired a grotesque-looking bulge around my middle where the girdle almost instantly slid up and settled in a bunch, I experienced unbelievable pain and discomfort because that rubber torture device was cutting off my circulation, and my suffering was all for nothing because the wonder working girdle wasn't wonderful, working, or flattening my tummy!

Becoming a grown up was complicated and uncomfortable, and I wasn't sure I could survive it. Returning to my life as a tomboy was looking more and more appealing as I began facing the necessary requirements of female adulthood.

Perhaps the most frustrating feeling I experienced was that everyone else I knew appeared to be making the transition into the next stage so much more grace-fully than I. Other girls seemed capable of effortlessly and attractively arranging their hair into any style. Absolutely everyone else, I was sure, was born with a board-flat tummy. You see, during the girl-talk sessions I had been listening without hearing.

If I had been able to get outside of myself during that awkward period, I would have realized my friends were agonizing over their own personal flaws, real and imagined, just as I felt at the mercy of mine.

In truth, the grass on their side of the fence had as many weeds as mine, but as an insecure observer, I could only see others' physical qualities as the prizes I thought I needed. The girls with poker straight hair envied my curls because they didn't have them. Some with pale complexions would have welcomed the freckles I com-plained made my face look like an oatmeal cookie.

My tall friends wanted to be short, my blue-eyed friends wanted to be brown-eyed, my brown-haired friends wanted to be blonds. If I didn't have it, I thought I wanted or needed it.

I had to learn there is a distribution system that gives something to everyone, and it was my responsibility to creatively turn what I had received into something special. I wished my hair would turn under into a page boy style, or that I had a flat tummy. I wished I didn't have a round face with freckles, but they were part of my package.

When I learned to accept that simple truth, that the grass just looked greener on the other side, my real tran-sition into adulthood began.

I finally learned my hair was acceptable even if it wasn't in a page boy . . . and at that time in my life, the only thing a girdle was good for was making a slingshot.

CROSSING LINES BETWEEN REALITY & OPTIMISM
—February 7, 1995

I've spent an inordinate amount of time attempting to do things that defy sensibility simply because I often think I don't need logical, explainable reasons for everything.

Such was the case when I decided to cross stitch a table cloth. It isn't counted cross stitch, because I don't count anything. I simply follow countless little blue crosses stamped on a fabric . . . for miles! I don't even have a suitable table for what I hope will one day be a lovely bit of needle work, but I'm doing it anyway.

This inspired moment of visualizing the beautiful fruits of my handiwork occurred more than twenty-five years ago. I'm now approximately three-fourths finished. Using basic calculations, I should be done in about eight years!

I discovered long ago (but still frequently forget) that while some projects appear to have great appeal, in reality they're either harder than anticipated, take longer than imagined, or are downright boring.

I tend to view distances between places the same way. I describe a two and a half hour trip as though it's on the next street, ignoring the time it takes to cross four counties and a state line.

My husband teases me about how I visualize finished products with little regard for the detailed steps involved in getting to them, especially if I'm not doing the work.

Whenever I begin to rationalize about the simplicity of any project with phrases like, "How hard can it be?" or "It won't take that long," my husband's eyes roll upward. If he hears, "We can replace the kitchen floor in a day," "We can lay railroad ties along there," or "We can just slide in a new shower stall," he gets nervous. Whenever I use the word "we" in this context we both know I really mean mostly "he."

Years of experience have taught him that, about some things, I pay no attention to details. I merely overlook them and assume wonderful things will just happen. Not so with this cross stitching business. I'm strictly on my own this time, and it isn't "just happening."

After a very brief period of sitting and covering little lines, I find my needle wandering all around the table cloth in haphazard fashion, at times trying to see how far I can go making only half-crosses before I either forget where I started or run out of embroidery floss. No one will ever be allowed to see the back of this cloth!

Even when I'm not wandering out of boredom, I've found I cross stitch the same way I play bridge, planning only one or two moves ahead. As a result, I often complete a small area only to discover three little naked blue crosses four inches away, without a single thread covering them!

After staring off and on at this same project for so many years, I've decided the Olympic Committee should open the competition to serious cross stitchers because they have a skill worthy of gold medals. They deserve recognition for displaying the tenacity and discipline of any athlete.

Just being able to successfully separate the floss should earn them high marks. Those manufacturers could sell it already separated for us but, no, they apparently enjoy the vision of people struggling with tangled strands!

At one point, I seriously entertained the notion that calculating the number of little crosses might be more interesting than trying to cover them, but decided there probably are googols (one of those words I've always wanted to use) and I don't need frustration compounding my boredom.

As he looked at my dubious work of art in the making, my husband asked if the puckers would come out when the cloth is finished. What a diabolical combination of pessimism and optimism. He doubts if those puckers will come out, but he honestly believes I'm going to finish the cloth!

At this point, unfortunately, the puckers are not what I'm worried about coming out. I want the miles of little blue crosses to wash out, since my aim is so poor many are still highly visible. However, I fear by the time I reach the washing stage, the embroidery floss will be so rotten and the blue dye so permanent the print will stay and the stitches will fall out. Covering the googols of little crosses will have been for naught.

Obviously, I can't predict whether or not this table cloth is going to be completed before the next century— well, yes I can, no it won't—but I will dabble for a while longer. When I can't bear to look at it for one more second, I'll put it aside for another extended period of time. It will remain stored until some strange notion moves me to try to finish before it (or I) becomes an antique.

I could hire someone to finish it for me, but I might have to explain why I started such a project in the first place. And that person would see the back, which resembles a seriously advanced condition of varicose veins. Worse, she might not be able to distinguish the back from the front.

Heck, I'll work on it for another eight years. Perhaps by then I may even remember why I started it in the first place. . . . Then again, what I may remember is I never did have a reason, only my usual vision of another finished product.

PARENTHOOD IS FOREVER—JULY 24, 1996

As contrary as it may sound, some endeavors never were meant to be completed.

As we drove to Columbus one fine morning, my husband noted he was experiencing feelings of *deja vu*. It was the familiarity of the routine more than anything else. We rode along in the truck with the trailer in tow, chuckling at how frequently we find ourselves in the roles of Ma and Pa Kettle, taking furniture or belongings to our children.

We went off to college with all our possessions in the trunk of the car, but that was before in-room televisions, stereos, couches, lofts, refrigerators, even microwaves.

Somehow, we survived those years of transporting our offspring to college, only to have them followed by more moves into apartments in different cities where their jobs took them. Gradually, just the truck was not adequate for these moves. Each successive relocation increased the amount of personal and household effects, requiring the truck, the trailer, a carload, and more often than not, several trips.

As we continued the first hour of our drive that particular day, we mused about how children come into and take control of their parents' lives. They arrive in this world as such small bundles, without even the shirts on their backs, which, obviously, changes dramatically the day they are brought home from the hospital.

All their needs and wishes become the ongoing goals and focal points of their parents. Their acquisitions overflow into every room. How such tiny beings can be such dominant figures has to be one of life's unsolved mysteries.

Right from the first day the pervading atmosphere was that there never was life without children. We barely can imagine what we did, where we went, what we talked about or were concerned with before our children were born. They added an indescribable dimension to our lives.

Perhaps one of the most amazing aspects of becoming a parent is that it has to be done without the benefit of manuals, warranties, money-back guarantees, thirty-day trial periods, or even care instructions printed on a label somewhere on this little package.

We made our usual coffee stop at the half-way point of our journey, got back on the road, and continued wondering about how and when we arrived at this point in our lives.

We thought again, in amazement, how growing into a family just happened, day by day. We were quite unaware of what this meant fully until we found ourselves with extra bedrooms; the kids had grown up and gone out on their own.

It just happened, like so many other things, and we realized we should begin preparing ourselves for the dreaded empty-nest syndrome, but it never came. We had the empty rooms, but not the empty house.

Somebody always seemed to need something that was still housed with us (apartments have limited space), or wanted to store something with us (apartments have limited space). As their living quarters grew, we tried to convince them to relieve us of some furnishings, theirs and/or ours.

It was then we discovered their tastes had changed

significantly enough so that many of the accumulated possessions had become white elephants no one wanted.

However, we have incurable pack rat tendencies, so nothing was ever disposed of . . . "one of us/them might need it." How else could I explain four couches in our house!

As we drove the last leg of the trip, my husband and I laughed as we recalled one summer day a year earlier when we felt ambitious, and desperate, and decided to organize our children's belongings still housed with us. We scoured the attic, the basement, their old rooms and the closets, and began to assign areas in the crawl space to each child. Anything that fit went in, but it was still like putting a band-aid on an amputation.

Cars and their various parts were still stored in the outbuildings. The remnants of years of owning a horse were, for the most part, still in and around the barn. We often threatened to move from here ourselves, but just the thought was overpowering and discouraging enough to keep us from taking immediate action, even knowing someday we would have to relocate.

After two hours of reminiscing about how often we find ourselves doing this very same thing, we arrived in Columbus with the latest shipment for our daughter. We visited, ate, and laughed about our adventures as movers. When the trailer was reloaded with the return cargo to be stored until further notice, we headed for home. We could only smile, knowing full well we would undoubtedly be doing this again.

Kids leave home and go off on their own, to lead their own lives and become independent, responsible adults, but they never lose a little part of them that always will be our little kids, no matter how hard they may try. They leave, but they never go away. Signing on as a parent is a permanent commitment, from the moment of your children's births until forever, and we wouldn't want it any other way.

Eventually, they will come to collect all their things—from wherever we may be living. The house may then look emptier, but our hearts never will be.

As Little Kids Phase Into Adults
—September 1, 1996

As I sat bleary-eyed and fighting to stay awake feeding an infant in the middle of the night, all the parental love in the world couldn't keep me from wondering how soon my baby would be old enough to be past that exhausting phase.

At the sight of a first tooth I ran for the camera, but the ongoing discomfort of teething made both mother and child anxious to be done with the process. Each new development in the children's lives brought first an excitement, followed soon by a desire for it to be over.

I looked forward to each new phase, even with its down sides, but somehow overlooked the reality that each one was, in fact, bringing my children a step closer to adulthood.

The irony is they began growing toward maturity the minute they arrived, but I was so busy measuring that growth by how short their pants and shoes became I missed many of the changes as they were happening.

Then one day I realized I was no longer preparing meals at odd times, doing laundry at the beginning and ending of every day, working full time, attending every season's ball games, keeping regular appointments with the orthodontist, and attending plays, choir, and band concerts. Suddenly I had time because my children had grown up.

The long list of signs had been growing, but I hadn't been paying attention. As I reviewed the signs, I knew that, for a long time, I'd been taking many of them for granted:

They stopped making collect calls so many years ago I don't even know for sure when it happened.

They call even when they have no requests for anything except to ask how we're doing and say hello.

They frequently discuss such mundane topics as mowing lawns, raking leaves, care of flower beds, the latest tractor malfunctions, how to prevent mildew in the shower, trying to remember recipes for favorite dishes, our deep snow and frigid temperatures, their high humidity and intense heat, and the dysfunctional garage door opener.

They tolerate my inability (still) to set the VCR or use a fax, things they do as easily as turning on the television set.

They admit now they do some of the very things I did that used to exasperate them when they were younger.

They worry about treating snow mold on their lawns.

They don't classify us as weird because we aren't interested in having cable television.

They use store coupons when they grocery shop.

They regard having learned to discriminately shop at the discount stores for bargains as a useful lesson.

They acknowledge that a new roof or gutters take precedence over a vacation, or at least alters its extent.

They are as repulsed as I when they hear the words (entertainer) Madonna and motherhood used in the same context.

They often say thanks and tell us we were right about something.

They prepare meals with foods they never would eat at home, or with foods I've never even heard of.

They do the driving when we travel somewhere together in a car, and I prefer it that way.

They know more about my car than I do.

They let us drive their cars.

They share a problem with us after they've solved it.

They dress appropriately without my supervision or suggestions about their appearances.

They enjoy many of the same television programs.

They agree with us about many current styles and trends.

They make better clothing selections for us than we make for ourselves.

They can be reached almost anywhere, any time, because of home and office addresses and phone numbers, along with their voice mail, e-mail, fax, pager, and car phone numbers. (We keep a separate directory just for them!)

Some people contend that, in spite of all other behaviors, if your children still have things stored in your house, they aren't fully grown up. That may or may not be so, I haven't decided yet. But if it's true, then I'm grateful.

We have some things stored our children haven't yet moved to their own homes. As long as they have anything here, I can legitimately think of them as "the kids." I know they're grown-ups, but in a parent's heart, there is always a little place reserved "for kids only."

Besides, those things serve to remind us of the up sides of each past phase.

MARRIAGE DISCOVERIES CONTINUE WITH AGE
—JUNE 27, 1995

With our children off on their own, my husband and I, as just a couple, have entered yet another phase: retirement living. It's a difficult concept to explain to anyone not yet fortunate enough to experience it first hand.

It's easier than going off to work every day, and its rewards and benefits are many, but it's not without some small hurdles and adjustments. The energy that previously had been directed at performing rather demanding jobs have had to be reexamined and refocused.

When close friends of ours, Ruth and Chuck, were on the threshold of retiring, they asked us if we argue now that we're both home all the time. Without hesitation we laughed and replied: *"Oh, Yeah!"*

Upon reconsideration, and in all fairness to us, I want to emend that statement. *We* don't argue—we make discoveries. We've changed from the two people who entered into this union more than four decades ago; frequently, the terms of the original contract are pushed to the limit.

After years of working full time, raising children, and being as involved outside the home as we were inside, we are gradually learning to refocus. The problem is, we don't always have the same target in our sights. And when we have, we don't always agree on how to hit it.

We've always known and accepted if there are two approaches to something, we will not choose the same one. Something as simple as walking away from the car—one goes around the front, the other around the back, but — and this is what matters—we arrive at the same place.

We have cousins who also recently retired. The

husband, a former Navy career officer, was accustomed to giving specific, unquestioned commands. The wife, a mother of five, was equally accustomed to issuing orders and directives.

They retired, moved to Florida, and promptly got in each other's faces. A lot! Two chiefs with no Indians! Demarcation lines have gradually been drawn, but it's hard to stop taking charge. It's even harder to convince others you don't want to be taken charge of!

Usually people must accept their job schedules, leaving little room for exercising personal choices and freedoms. When that option finally does become available, it can be overwhelming, and deciding how to use it can be puzzling at times. We've always known I'm more of a private person, but even I didn't realize how private until I found myself almost never being alone.

My reactions have bordered on territorial. For instance, what was once simply my kitchen has now become *my kitchen*, and I've developed a pretty convincing "don't-even-think-about-it!" look to prove it.

The automobile, however, has been one of the major focal points in our period of settling into this new life.

We're learning how to go almost everywhere in the same car, something we seldom did before. On those occasions when we did travel together, my husband always drove. Neither of us could remember the last time he was the passenger when I drove. In this new scheme of things, *that* had to change.

It wasn't part of Plan A, but in the early stages of developing a "share-the-driving" routine, he broke some ribs and we were forced to resort to a total reversal—I did *all* the driving.

Truth: I nearly drove him nuts! He was amazed to learn how conservatively I drive. He'd been forced into the passenger seat and had to be chauffeured by a wimpy little old lady!

Our different driving styles (among other things) notwithstanding, we now acknowledge that we each prefer to be the driver. Bottom line: we're both lousy passengers.

After he mended sufficiently, we reverted back to Plan A, a satisfactory compromise, and now take turns, but it's interesting to note how capably either of us can drive from anywhere in the car, with or without the steering wheel, verbally, or by using only body language. Our combined driving skills are required to get us to our destinations. I don't know how we went anywhere alone before. Compromise is not only possible, it's absolutely vital for survival!

Some days I feel as though we're newly-weds, just learning about each other. He didn't have the slightest idea how, or how often, I do laundry, and I've (finally) discovered he doesn't like cinnamon. When we're folding a drop cloth (or any other large cloth) after we've finished painting a room (he prefers a roller, I a brush), we still bring up the opposite sides on the first try.

In spite of these adjustments, I confess I like the new version of my mate as well as, or better than, the original, but we communicate differently, in part thanks to Ruth.

We keep two humorous posters she once gave us close at hand. When I begin to feel crowded, I point to the one that reads, I HAVE ONE NERVE LEFT AND YOU'RE GETTING ON IT! When my husband has had enough of my attitude, he waves his slogan at me: 51% SWEETHEART, 49% B_ _ _ _; DON'T PUSH IT!

I made copies to give back to Ruth and Chuck, in case they've misplaced theirs!

Updating An Old Memory—March 1, 1997

Memories are among the things that get lost from time to time, or at least become selective and personalized. Ten people may attend the same party, but what each will recall, shortly thereafter or many years later, will be uniquely individual.

Not only may your recollections and reconstruction of the past not agree with others', you might find time and change distort your own images.

Trying to relive memories seems to be a sure-fire way of discovering they're never quite the same as we remember, but that rarely stops us from trying to recapture the first taste of an Eskimo Pie or a lemon ice all over again.

In a moment that is as spontaneous as it gets for us, my husband and I drove up to Niagara Falls. We hadn't been there in twenty years but it was hard to imagine there would be much change in such a magnificent natural creation.

We stopped at the Canadian border and dutifully answered the guard's questions. When he asked if we had anything to declare, we couldn't resist declaring "it certainly was a beautiful day." However, he did not share in our enthusiasm. After repeating his short litany of questions so often, he was apparently in no mood for cute comments. He made no unpleasant reply, but rolled his eyes and waved us through. We, on the other hand, would not be discouraged by his dismissal. We were in search of a memory.

I was anxious to eat at The Refectory, to buy that mouth-watering English toffee, to see the sparkle of the Falls at night when the lights are turned on. It was all going to be such a wonderful adventure.

Because it was off season, my first surprise was the emptiness of the entire area, but I adjusted quickly since I don't do well in crowds anyway. Interestingly, while there were very few tourists, there also was a limited number of local residents about. It was eerie at first, but pleasant when we realized we could walk everywhere without rubbing elbows with anyone or waiting in line anywhere.

The next obvious difference was the increased number of motels, restaurants, and places of entertainment and amusement tightly packed around the Falls. Many were not yet open for the season, but their marquees promised comfortable, affordable accommodations, a wide variety of delicious foods, and unlimited fun for the whole family.

To my dismay, The Refectory had been replaced by Queen Victoria Park, and fudge, not toffee, seemed to be the candy of choice sold almost everywhere.

Our eleventh floor hotel room was in a five-year old building. Since nothing was yet in bloom, we could see the Falls through the bare tree branches that would otherwise obstruct the view during the season. That part was lovely.

However, I experienced yet another disappointment when the spotlights were turned on at night. We could barely see the Falls, either from our room, or when standing right alongside the stone wall that guards them. I think I've seen birthday candles give off more of a glow. The glow certainly did not match my stored image.

We had a close-up view of the Skylon from the room. On the family trip we had traveled in fascination to the top to dine, spin, and gaze in awe out over the city. The external elevators once reminded me of big, yellow gumballs rolling out of that tower. On this trip I viewed them as big, yellow vitamin capsules, sliding up and down, day and night, again and again. Perhaps that's a difference between youth and "maturity." It was the same, but not really.

While there, we talked by phone with our daughter and mentioned returning to some of the places we had visited as a family. Obviously, it was before she had begun actively storing memory since so little sounded familiar to her. That stirred questions in me. What makes something a memory to one person but completely deserts another?

In recalling events from her own youth, my mother often noted there was hardly anyone left to either refute or support her memories. She couldn't compare notes to determine if she remembered the way it was or as she wanted it to be. Suddenly I understood.

Niagara Falls was still there, but our old memories were not. They were still back in the first edition, securely saved. What we did instead of finding the old memories was write a new version, a revised edition, to be mentally stored next to the original. We will probably compare them once in awhile, but they really are not comparable. Keep some, lose some, adjust many.

On the trip home we stopped at a grocery store where I saw something else from my past: tempting, delicious-looking coconut and chocolate covered cake bars. I mentioned to my husband they were a treat when I was a kid and how much I used to love them. Then I walked away. Surprised, he asked why I didn't buy them if I liked them so much.

I told him I wasn't ready to taste the updated edition of that memory yet.

THE AGING OF WINE, CHEESE, AND MEMORIES
—JULY 21,1998

Recently a cousin and I had the opportunity to visit after not having seen each other for thirty years. We'd both left the familiar area where we'd grown up together, lived in many different geographical locations, and somehow missed connecting at the usual family weddings and funerals.

Initially, the changes in our physical appearances, coupled with the fact we do have children in their late thirties and early forties, jolted me into a reality I don't always acknowledge—I felt as ancient as Methuselah.

However, I recovered sufficiently from the shock to get down to the serious business of filling in the spaces formed during those three decades with current news and happenings.

The occasion evoked thoughts about times and places stored in the far reaches of my mind, things I don't ponder on a daily basis, and, in the true pattern of reunion conversations, it wasn't long before we naturally switched from updating to "Do-you-remember-when...?" The most amazing aspect of our joint efforts to reconstruct the past was how differently we each remembered the same incidents.

The incident triggering a series of debatable stories took place in the church yard when we were in grade school and a nun caught us trying to play hooky from catechism class. The issue in question was not whether we were guilty of the accusation but rather how we attempted to dodge the bullet of punishment after being caught.

My memory clearly showed me, and only me, suffering the full wrath of Sister Bridget's wagging finger and sharp, condemning tongue in front of God and every kid I knew in the whole world. My cousin had somehow managed to slip away.

Instead of getting back into line after being duly singed by the fire and brimstone lecture, I literally escaped further chastisement when "Sister Penguin's" back was turned. Confident she wouldn't chase me, I bolted and caught up with my deserter cousin, who was halfway home.

My cousin's rendition, on the other hand, featured her heroically grabbing my arm and dragging me away to safety after Sister had soundly scolded and embarrassed both of us, at which time she had announced dramatically we didn't have to stay there and take that.

We never completely resolved which role each played in the histrionic encounter, but agreed we were equally stupid and had ultimately learned a lot from the experience, regardless of who was at fault.

So it went, one recollection instantly prompting another, embellished favorably by the story teller while sounding slightly discordant to the listener. In less than twenty-four hours we went from biased veterans with firm memories and no questions, to young whipper-snappers with all the answers unknowingly establishing those memories, back to comfortable adults with uncorroborated memories and none of the answers.

Yet, in spite of all the discussion and debate nothing changed. When my cousin left I'm sure she took her versions with her intact, just as I put mine back securely the way I'd found and prefer to keep them.

I reminded myself we're only as old or as smart as we feel, regardless of how much the years and other people's memories try to convince us otherwise. So much for feeling like Methuselah!

UPGRADING LIFE STYLE BY DOWN-SIZING
—OCTOBER 1, 1998

We all know the old song, *Who Could Ask For Anything More?* So, what more could a person possibly want: four rolling wooded acres bordered by ravines and a river; mature fruit and flowering trees, lush beds and banks of flowers and shrubs surrounding a grand older ten-room Dutch colonial with loads of charm and character; enough out buildings and garages to house five cars, yard equipment, a horse stall, and a large workshop.

Privacy. Prestige. Self-sufficiency.

High continuous maintenance. Never-ending work.

Listen carefully as I sing that refrain now: "Who could Ask For Anything Less?"

We could. We did.

It was not a decision made in haste, but when the time came, we recognized it. At the risk of sounding like an ingrate, the rewards of such bountiful living came through unending work that became more and more demanding each year.

The house and property were aging and requiring greater attention, but so were we. Like so many others of our generation, we had to decide where to spend our reserve of strength. It was time to make a decision.

We were not opting for inactivity, we were looking to redirect our energies towards activities that would cut us some slack, not be so pressing if they were not attended to within the confines of such strict time limits: trees that had to be pruned or sprayed at specific intervals; bushels of produce that could not be sinfully ignored; a minimum of five hours of weekly mowing that could not be neglected; branches and trees that had to be cleared, cut, and stacked.

Maintaining an appealing cosmetic appearance as well as a functional operation was personally important and vitally necessary, but keeping up with the daily nuts-and-bolts to make it all happen began to take its physical toll. Soon almost everything was second to the pervasive demands of "The Place." We were mentally incapable of turning over any of the responsibilities to anyone else. Either we did it all, or we did none. The difficult decision was made.

Life in a cluster home is not totally free of maintenance requirements, but they are less demanding, and the lines of ownership are drawn differently. Private landscaping and outdoor floral embellishments are greatly reduced in size but still offer the satisfaction of some personalized ornamentation, while the necessity of routine maintenance such as mowing is left in the capable hands of younger, stronger individuals.

Interior decor is still a choice but the painting and wallpapering usually cover far fewer, and often newer, walls than were left behind in the larger home.

We asked for less and have received more: more free time to read without guilt, more liberty to travel without involved advance preparations, and more mental and physical energy to direct towards new endeavors.

We are enjoying another new beginning, another opportunity to conquer a new set of primarily mental rather than physical challenges. It is an inviting revitalization.

I tend to draw parallels every time we redesign or make changes in our life styles, but the current living arrangement is best described when I compare it to my eating habits. My body now balks at large meals, and has physically convinced me I feel more comfortable and am just as satisfied when I appease it with smaller ones.

I knew it was time to believe my mind when it began preaching the same message as my body. It was time to understand and accept that less can be just as rewarding, perhaps even more so, at the appropriate time.

IN ONE YEAR AND OUT THE OTHER—MARCH 1, 1996

They must be here some place. I couldn't have just lost them without some clue as to where they went. They couldn't have simply disappeared into thin air. . . or, could they?

These are the curious sentiments I find myself expressing many days, and I'm not trying to find a pair of gloves or misplaced car keys. I'm trying to decide what happened to at least a quarter of a century. It was just here a few minutes ago, I'm sure.

My friend Karen and I visit by phone and letter, spending a great deal of the time exchanging news about mutual friends. Often that news involves people who are feeling under the weather with the current bug, feeling the draining effects of coping with their own or a loved one's serious illness, or worse, no longer feeling anything.

I don't mean to make light of reality, but we have traveled the long road for a good many years and are not strangers to the fact some of our peers are no longer up to traveling with us. As Karen so succinctly asked, "Weren't we just having wedding and baby showers? Why can't we even find time to meet for lunch?"

The rapid passage of time is not a new revelation. We have heard variations of that phrase repeated all of our lives, but we're always so busy dealing with the momentary difficulties and issues, we seldom stop long enough to enjoy the countless number of gifts put right in our paths, the very same gifts that disappear as quickly as time itself.

We conscientiously bathed and fed the little babies, then one day discovered it was nearly impossible to get them out of the shower in less than thirty minutes, or keep them away from the refrigerator for more than thirty minutes. In the blink of an eye we went from six ounces of formula every six hours to a gallon of milk every twenty-four. In between blinks, we really intended to find some time to meet for lunch with old and dear friends.

The toddlers who had to be kept under constant surveillance as they explored every drawer and tried to climb into every cupboard were suddenly being transported to kindergarten one morning by nervous mothers. What seemed like later that same afternoon, those little five-year-olds turned sixteen and transported themselves and all their friends to dances and to the mall. That was minutes, surely, before they marched across the stage to accept diplomas.

College, then jobs in distant cities beckoned. Home was where they were, not here. Now, when the phone rings, it isn't for one of them, we hope it is one of them.

Where did the years go? No one ever seems to have the answer to that question, even though everyone eventually asks it. Jim Croce wishfully sang of saving time in a bottle. He wasn't successful, of course, he knew it couldn't be done, but as young as he was, he realized how precious and elusive time is.

Time can't be saved, stopped, or stored. It is meant to be used fully at all times. Every moment I fail to seize is gone forever. Carpe diem.

There is some reassurance in knowing the time is there; it is I who must remind myself to be quick, and wise, enough to use and appreciate its worth. Then I wouldn't be so concerned with where it is or what I may have lost.

Too bad we can't keep track of time with an "idiot string," that curiously wonderful innovation that stretches between mittens from sleeve to sleeve through a coat. If we could, we might enjoy more and worry less about losing it. We might even fondly remember where those years are.

In the meantime, I must go call my friend and make arrangements to meet for lunch while we still recognize each other.

LESSONS FROM A GRAHAM CRACKER—JULY 22, 1997

Graham crackers have been around for generations. The crisp, Oh, so sweet and satisfying wafer, has become an interesting symbol to me, representing how some of life's simple little experiences actually teach very big important lessons. Even with all its versatile options, graham crackers teach that some basic things remain constant.

At a very early age I began working to master the fine art of dunking graham crackers in cold milk or hot chocolate—timing was everything! The challenge involved in trying to perfect this skill provided me with entertainment and a valuable lesson in patience.

For many years thereafter my experiences with graham crackers continued to expand. Eating them with a variety of both sensible and less than conventional spreads and toppings was another activity that occupied much of my time. Incidentally, dunking a topped cracker is not recommended.

The most disgusting topping I tried was ketchup. I was probably five at the time and I'm happy to say that unpalatable snack was eliminated after about three crackers. Mustard was never even a consideration. The lesson, developing discriminating taste in a variety of areas.

Shortly after this I entered my peanut butter and graham cracker phase which lasted for many years. Even now it comes to the rescue when I can't decide what to nibble.

That special combination is reminiscent of long talks and late nights when friends and I consumed it in large quantities to ward off certain starvation, the imagined fate of college students with no 'fridge to raid. Lesson: learn to recognize and rely on the tried and true.

Off and on I had graham crackers spread with apple butter—soggy, but okay in a pinch—if you ate quickly, or the seasonal treat, S'mores, but they only tasted right in front of a camp fire in autumn. Still another lesson, something with too many conditions can be hard to accept.

Commercially covered chocolate graham crackers were all right, but eating a graham cracker that came out of a package already covered with something I didn't put there was like breaking an unwritten rule. Lesson: if a rule is worth establishing, then I must be sure to follow it.

Briefly, I was into the frosting phase, lavishly slathering homemade and canned flavors on my honey graham crackers. However, as tasty as all the varieties were, when I began opening cans of frosting expressly for that purpose (as opposed to finishing a little that was left over), I had to rethink my snacking habit.

Important lesson: Be sure my motives are genuine and not overly self-serving.

All three of the above examples also taught me a lesson in recognizing fads or fancies when they came my way. Nowadays, my plain, simple honey graham crackers are eaten unadorned, straight out of the box. I've only recently realized how my graham cracker habit has come full circle, from the way it began and now back to that same state.

In a television commercial a voice says, "The more things change, the more things stay the same." No matter how often I hear those words, I ponder their meaning and usually arrive at the same conclusion, that many things in life go through a test before we accept that not everything must be changed to be good, another lesson worth remembering.

Sooner or later many of us discover yet another important lesson: that many things (some of seemingly small significance), will survive many changes, return to their original state, and demonstrate that our first introductions to them were really the best after all.

Does everything eventually come full circle before we learn to see and accept it for what it really is?

Just because we started life with no teeth, should we assume we'll one day return to a toothless state?

Can a little bald-headed baby automatically expect to become a little bald-headed old person?

If we learn to play well as a children, will we then remember how to do so again when our working years are done?

Does the youngster who learns to trust fully, and without question, keep enough of that faith through years of disappointing experiences and dishonest encounters to eventually become unquestionably trusting again?

I have no idea, but that doesn't disturb me. It only serves to teach me two more lessons: not all questions have obvious answers, or, in some cases, any answers at all, and making broad generalizations can be very unreliable when drawing conclusions.

Ah, but good old, plain honey graham crackers—they've come full circle through many changes and still remain the same—sweet, satisfying, just the way they were when I first learned to enjoy them. . . .

Dang! I wasn't paying attention—half my cracker fell into my milk! Now I have to start over again with another cracker.

Some of life's finer skills just require constant practice if we don't want to lose them, another invaluable lesson I occasionally forget.

Unconscious Transformations—July 1, 1998

The sepia-toned magazine advertisement showed a woman luxuriously indulging in a peaceful, quiet moment in a soothing bath. Beneath it was the question, "At exactly which point in our lives did a long, hot bath go from being the ultimate punishment to the ultimate reward?"

Don't ask me what was being advertised. I was too busy thinking, "Ain't *that* the truth!"

I like to think I control what I do, that I'm aware of what is going on around me at all times, and that I consciously decide when to continue or abandon certain behaviors and attitudes. It sounds good in theory, but in practice, I know better.

Even armed with that knowledge, it's still occasionally surprising when I discover some of my reactions have done a one-eighty and I don't remember when, why, or how. In retrospect, I'm inclined to think I've gone from zero to sixty-plus a lot like Topsy: "I just growed!"

Much can be attributed to simply growing up, I'm sure. Perhaps because as a youngster I was always wishing I would hurry up and be old enough to do specific things, my singular focus was narrower than I realized, and normal changes went unnoticed without my immediate awareness.

For example, I was so busy concentrating on being the best baseball player in the neighborhood, it came as something of a rude awakening when one day into my late teens I came across my old mitt and cap and couldn't even remember when I'd last worn them. Suddenly I knew I had at some point done what would have been unthinkable as a pre-teenager—abandoned my status as a tomboy.

Without conscious recollection of actually doing so, I had exchanged my mitt and one less-than-neatly-groomed phase in my life for a purse in which to carry a comb and lipstick that I used regularly to improve my appearance, and didn't even recall going through the transition. What's more, the thought of constantly having been dirt-smudged, uncombed, and unlady like was almost unimaginable.

That explanation seems appropriate enough for the very young, but I went into adulthood still experiencing belated awareness about my attitudinal changes.

As a young adult I often staunchly announced I'd never adopt certain maternal behaviors when I grew older. I guess I grew older—the calendar certainly would have me believing so—because one day I looked in the mirror and saw that I'd become my mother.

I'm not sure how or when I crossed over into maturity so completely, and I'm pretty sure I didn't have a written script to practice, or even a dress rehearsal to prepare me, yet I now notice I'm naturally and comfortably doing many of the things I swore I'd never do. Curiously, I don't remember why I was so bent on avoiding them.

This mysterious transformation process, causing me to view the same phases from different ages with such diversely opposing attitudes, has apparently taken place my entire life and I've never been alert enough to catch it as it was going on. Even now, knowing it is going to happen again, will not prevent me from being bewildered when I recognize another change of attitude long after the fact.

The one thing I have decided is growing up like Topsy is not all bad. She never knew exactly how she got where she was, but it wasn't a particular hindrance to her. Evidently she accepted that some things simply happened and she was okay with that.

Maybe more important than understanding how we grow from one attitude into another, or knowing how we get to each stage, is what we do with that time while we're there.

I might have to indulge myself in a soothing, relaxing bubble bath to ponder the possibilities. And when I do, I think I'll wear my old baseball cap as I do so, just for old times' sake.

Carpe diem!

IT'S FINALLY TIME TO PLAY—JULY 1, 1999

Usually, they are easy to identify. Perhaps you know a few yourself.

They travel the highway in a sporty, candy-apple red two-seater convertible with the top down. Her forty dollar salon "do" is replaced by one that "does" what it wants. His hair, or what's left of it, is in total disarray. They're smiling.

They sail the lakes and rivers, perhaps wearing matching captain's caps and natty looking cut-offs, ignoring their slightly expanding mid-sections while concentrating on developing rich tans instead. They are relaxed.

He cruises the electronics stores, stays informed, up-to-date, and well supplied with every new gadget to complement and/or upgrade the computer, home and car stereo sound systems, surround-sound big screen television and VCR, and anti-theft alarms that would summon the National Guard. He buys new tools because they're *cool*.

She cruises the kitchenware shops, compares mushroom slicers, vegetable steamers, espresso makers, gadgets for cleverly changing radishes and carrots into flowers, and machines for producing fifteen varieties of pasta, even though at home she rarely does more than brew coffee or heat up the contents of restaurant doggie bags in the microwave. She buys new kitchen tools because they match her kitchen.

They play as fiercely and competitively as the younger week-end warriors. They engage in pick-up ball games, golf and bowling leagues, and tennis and racquetball matches, followed by trips to the gym in case any body parts weren't adequately exercised while playing. Maintaining peak physical condition is a priority, even though there's more physique to maintain and the peak is slightly elusive.

Both wear jewelry. He complements the standard gold wedding band with a distinctive-looking ring or two, a small, plain gold necklace, perhaps even sports a Rolex watch. She wears several bracelets, three pairs of earrings, rings on almost every finger, gold chains, and a lapel pin or two, one of which is usually an angel. They check in at airports an extra hour early in order to clear security.

Their hobby is collecting, anything from buttons to beer cans. They spend hours scouring junk shops, flea markets, and garage sales in search of potential valuables. They plan their excursions around interesting restaurants.

They have a need to at least "try on for size" the expensive sport utility vehicles, motor homes, "trendy" clothing, and anything operated with a remote control transmitter. They window shop frequently.

Some would diagnose these activities as the classic symptoms of Second Childhood—an affliction often associated with retirees accused of being afraid to age. I beg to differ with that diagnosis.

I believe it's a state of awareness, not fear. Those alert enough to enter this phase with such gusto recognize an open window of opportunity. They finally, and legitimately, can enjoy themselves without feeling guilty.

The current generation of recycled teenagers spent little time, or anything else, on themselves. Many began working, marrying, and raising children at an early age, a choice and commitment which they honored and in all probability would make again. Now they've earned recess.

It's finally their time to play while they still can find some pleasure in doing so. For many of these so-called indulgent individuals, this is not a Second Childhood— it's the first legitimate one they've ever had.

The only prescribed requirement: Enjoy the rewards!

CHOCOLATE CHIP REWARDS—MAY 16, 1995

It is generally accepted that being well-adjusted is an admirable, but often elusive, quality that cannot always be as successfully mastered as would be desirable. It's a rather ambiguous term that often applies to people who quietly make the best of difficult or unwelcome situations.

People who eat yellow jelly beans without fussing are well-adjusted as far as I'm concerned. I personally go to great lengths to avoid them until I have no other options.

Clearly, just accepting the yellow jelly beans along with the more favorite flavors isn't the ultimate proof a person is well-adjusted. There are many other, far more serious demonstrations that give credibility to this desirable attribute. A friend shared a story with me that moved her and her family right to the top of my list of well-adjusted people.

In the twenty plus years I've known Val, there never has been any doubt she is fortunate enough to belong to a truly close, loving family, a closeness that embraces all generations equally. It was with great sorrow when I learned her grandmother had passed away, a sorrow which in no way matched that of the family's. Grandma was quite a gal!

In her final hours of life she remained positive and was genuinely interested in everything the family did.

Upon learning some of the great-grandchildren had a trampoline, she expressed the wish that she could play on it with them.

From across the room she overheard someone suggest she probably meant she wished she could watch them playing on it. The mentally alert, ninety-something woman chuckled and corrected the well-meaning interpreter—she had said what she meant—she wanted to play! Given the opportunity, she would have at least sat and bounced on it, I'm sure.

Shortly thereafter, she slid quietly to her final rest.

There was, of course, sadness during the period of visitation and at the funeral service when people came to pay respects. But this woman's love of life and her sense of humor had not been lost on her family, especially granddaughter Val and Val's brother.

As they stood at the casket looking at this beloved woman with whom they had shared so much, seeing her hands crossed in peaceful repose, they were both suddenly moved to act on an idea that, somehow, surely must have come as a direct request from Grandma.

That was early in July.

Later in the year, having to go through the holidays for the first time without Grandma was difficult, but everyone remembered her favorably with smiles and humorous anecdotes. As family members gathered to visit one quiet evening, a plate of cookies was being passed. Someone lifted a chocolate chip cookie in tribute and announced, "This one's for Grandma!"

Although they are grown adults, Val and her brother momentarily assumed the roles of little kids, looked at each other with a shared sense of guilt that was then followed by uncontrollable laughter. They could no longer keep the secret they had shared since the funeral.

Their mother had to be told Grandma took her chocolate chip cookies with her.

Shortly before the casket was closed Val and her brother had slipped some of the cookies she so passionately loved into Grandma's hands. It seemed fitting she get to take along one of the treats she so enjoyed, one of the few things that could go with her.

At first they weren't sure how to interpret their mother's reaction to this news. It was just possible that in her brief silence following this revelation she felt they had crossed the line from humor into disrespect. After all, these "kids" who had pulled off this caper are responsible, forty-something parents themselves and should have acted accordingly by setting good examples.

But they should have realized the love, combined with the sense of humor that makes this family so close, is in all of them, and especially in their mother. After all, she's Grandma's daughter! Without exception, they all laughed heartily and agreed that Grandma, the best example-setter of them all, would have been the first to laugh. In a way, she also got the last laugh!

Certainly, many people achieve some measure of being well-adjusted through various methods—a sense of humor is but one of those ways. Val's family has that admirable quality we refer to as being well-adjusted, and a warm sense of humor has surely contributed greatly to sustaining it.

Garrison Keillor said, "Humor is not a trick, not jokes. Humor is a presence in the world—like grace—and shines on everybody." Grandma could not have bestowed anything greater on her family.

You know, I'll bet she ate the yellow jelly beans without complaining, too, but she probably ate them first, just so she could enjoy her favorite flavors at the end.

KEEPING AN IMPORTANT CONNECTION
—AUGUST 25, 1998

Bret Nicholaus and Paul Lowrie wrote "The Conversation Piece," a little book filled with questions to spark variations on "what if" thoughts. One question in particular set me thinking: "What is one item you own that you really should throw away . . . but probably never will?"

I am a selective saver, therefore I don't number myself among the serious pack rats who collect anything attainable and/or portable. I understand the thinking of those who subscribe to the theory that almost anything could become valuable someday, but I choose not to devote that much time, energy, or storage space to such a remote possibility.

As a result, I altered the question for the benefit of some personal pondering: "Even though I'm not a true saver, what is the one item I'll probably never throw away?" My musings took me almost immediately to my mother.

She never would have been identified as a saver, although a few special keepsakes were of great importance to her. As I sorted through her belongings, it was very easy to separate those things that would readily become disposables from those that were going to find their way into my home and my life, and continue to be special for at least one more generation. Monetary worth would not be a factor in the decision-making process.

Among the treasured articles were meaningful mementos from times she and my dad shared; some memorabilia marking significant times and events in my own childhood and growing years; early hand-crafted gifts, then specially purchased ones from her only two grandchildren, accompanied by notes written in childish scrawl that gradually developed into more personal and mature script as they grew.

There were a limited number of things from her own childhood, but perhaps the most important was the rocker she inherited from the mother she knew less than eight years.

The simple walnut chair with five spindles on the back is quite small, but then, she and her mother were small people so this piece of furniture was well suited to them. The unpadded cracked seat and arms were worn smooth down to the bare wood from hours of sitting for more than a century.

For years the little chair occupied a corner of her bedroom and served as a quiet refuge to which she could retreat from her active life for a few minutes of peaceful solitude to regroup and prepare for the constant busyness of daily obligations during her young and middle-aged years.

In her seventies and eighties, she gradually began showing signs of slowing down, and in her later widowed years, she moved the rocker to the living room where it became her vantage point from which to better observe what was happening in her familiar surroundings, as well as her place of comfort and contemplation. It was also the place where she spent her final minutes.

While they provide pleasant memories and interesting anecdotes, most of the objects from my mother are nothing more than adjuncts. I plan to keep these personal possessions, and, yes, I would miss them if for some reason I felt compelled to part with them, but the space they would leave would eventually be filled in with other things, and the memories they've created would sustain me.

Not so with the little rocker. It is part of an image that represents a haven of security when I was a small child, an association with a place free from tension, an island refuge in a sometimes chaotic world.

Its absence would create a void nothing else would be able to fill. It is more than a representative of years gone by. It is the one tangible item that permanently, physically connects me to my mother.

Dignifying the Game of Independence
—December 16, 1995

Describing my mother as an independent person was spoken as a compliment. The description carried with it positive reflections of a woman who admirably, and successfully, constantly remained responsible for her own actions and well-being. It was an art, requiring a certain, subtle skill to maintain that position her entire life.

After my dad passed away in the spring of 1977, we were, naturally, concerned about my mom. That she always had been very independent and more than capable of taking care of herself seemed immaterial. We were uncomfortable leaving her on her own. The knowledge that most people face that possibility at some time was inconsequential.

The distance between her home and ours was just far enough to be worrisome, but she was adamant in her decision to remain where she was. Because of the pros and cons regarding how much or how little widowed parents should be coerced into leaving their familiar surroundings, we reluctantly agreed to give her as much time as she needed to decide when she could comfortably leave her home. We hoped she would be able to decide soon.

I often spoke with local widowed friends, members of my mother's generation, who always said the same thing when I expressed my concerns: "Let her stay in her own home." I tried to heed their advice, but it was difficult, so I continued to bring up the subject of her relocating.

It was years before I realized that, intentionally or otherwise, she'd made a game of the subject. Each spring, in response to our request, she would encourage us to check into possible housing options in our area. She would come to look them over, but that was all she did, and she rarely stayed more than three days. Independent people always have to get back home. They always have "things" to do.

Somehow the summer would slide into Labor Day. Jerry Lewis' telethon officially ended the season, but, according to my mother, it also heralded the beginning of the holiday season. She couldn't move during "the holidays." We'd just have to wait until afterward to think about making a change. (Queen to rook, check.) She played the game so well.

January and winter would come, but she couldn't move then. She'd prefer to wait until spring, when the weather would be better. About mid-winter she would initiate serious discussions about moving, assuring us she'd be ready to make major changes in her lifestyle soon. The queen subtly maneuvered bishops, pawns, knights, and, yes, castles with such skill. (Check, and check again.)

The game went on for years, played by her rules, and each season brought the predictable moves. After coming full circle, she would start again by agreeing to look at the offerings in the spring. Everything would be suitable except . . .

Her reasons for backing down were all legitimate. She had: good neighbors and friends, readily available bus service, easy access to her doctors, familiarity within her own surroundings, but most important of all—she had independence.

That alone gave her the impetus to remain active and to maintain her dignity. Concern for her notwithstanding, the game would be played by her rules.

In the spring of 1995, the game ended the way she probably knew it should. She had played masterfully right to the end and ultimately had won the victory when she did, in fact, change her lifestyle and leave her home for good—on her terms, with her independence and her dignity still intact. (Queen to King. Checkmate!)

Close the Door When You Leave
—August 20, 1995

The group was the same one I had known and worked with for many years, getting together at the end of another summer break to have lunch and prepare for the opening of the coming school year. It had become customary to do so, an occasion to celebrate mutual anticipation of new and exciting challenges, commiseration over some problems which never appear to be resolved, and preparation for meeting whatever unknowns waited ahead.

I met the others at the appointed time and place and immediately felt the pleasures one experiences when seeing old friends after a lengthy separation. With everyone seemingly talking at the same time, there were the usual warm greetings, exchanges of pictures from weddings, vacations, new babies or grandchildren, and a general updating of what everyone had been doing for the past couple of months. After that, the conversations quickly turned to the coming year.

That was when I was once again reminded that two years earlier I had walked out the door of the school building as a teacher for the last time. Only now was I beginning to realize I had neglected to close that door behind me. I was not returning to my classroom to do the job I had done for thirty-some years. I no longer had an active role in the planning and preparation of the goals towards which the others would be dedicating themselves. I had become an outsider, almost a spectator. It was a strange sensation.

The sensation was strange, but not devoid of an enthusiasm of a uniquely different nature. Even though I knew all but a few of the newer teachers, our paths would not cross in the same meaningful way as they once had. We now went in separate directions, they to continue with their educational careers, and I to move on to other new and interesting endeavors.

After hearing any available news of former students those present were able to share with me, I found myself knowing very little about the other business being discussed: new staff, new programs, new materials, new schedules. I was no longer a part of that world.

Doors are so symbolic of the journey through life. Long before we understand phrases referring to opportunities that knock on them, we begin the passage through a continual series of doors. They seem to represent the beginnings and endings of each phase of life as we experience it, the openings and closings, if you will.

There is no particular set pattern or number through which one must pass in order to achieve the various levels of growing and learning, and certainly we do not all choose to go through the same doors, but the symbolism remains intact: to constantly enter new stages in our lives.

There seems to be a built-in sense that tells us when we have seen and learned as much as we can after passing through each door, a sense that indicates it's time to move on through another door.

As the afternoon progressed I felt more and more detached from that time in my life, but I had resisted fully closing that door because it had been so easy to slip back; the friendships were so good and longstanding. What I realized was I could close the door behind me without losing what I had gained while on the other side of it. The friendships of so many years would always be there, but that period of my life had been fulfilled and it was time to experience something new.

It is said you can't go back in time, you can only go forward, but that does not mean you can't take with you what you have learned and loved from any given time into the next phase of your life. Anything and everything that is experienced contributes another part to the makeup of the whole person, hopefully adding to the enrichment of life.

When I left to return home that day I knew I would be able to close that door without any losses. I would be keeping with me years of good memories and warm feelings that were a permanent part of me. I had spent the afternoon looking at a piece of the past, and without a past, there is no future.

Now my built-in sense was working to the fullest, telling me it was okay to close the door to that time. It's very important to close the doors when you decide to move on.

Just be sure you don't lock them.

ABOUT THE AUTHOR

For more than thirty years, Angela Huston taught school and in Texas and Ohio, developing a successful program for students with learning disabilities and being named Teacher of the Year at Huntington School in the Brunswick City School System. She retired in 1990 and shifted her focus to freelance writing. Since 1992, she has contributed regular columns to *Medina County Gazette* (Medina, Ohio), *Focus* (Akron, Ohio), *Women's Press* (Akron, Ohio) *Times of Your Life* (Cuyahoga County, Ohio), and *Horizons* (Wayne County, Ohio). Her columns range from reflective essays and feature stories on local people and places, to restaurant and theater reviews and area social news. Huston's articles have also appeared in *Ohio Family, Sun Newspapers, The Plain Dealer,* and *Over the Back Fence.* **Looking Through Rose-Tinted Bifocals** is her first book.

"I've served on every committee known to motherhood," says Huston, "and I would do it all again in a heartbeat!" Huston is also proud to say she's "baked about a kajillion cookies and put up at least that many jars of canned goods. Now, she admits, we eat out!"